IN MEMORY OF

RENEE NICOLE GOOD

A BEARER OF WITNESS

BEARING WITNESS
POEMS FOR TROUBLED TIMES

Cover art by Sarah Yeoman

Book design by Alan Abrams

ISBN: 979-8-9992568-8-1

Library of Congress Control Number: 00000000000*
*Application # 1-15061870941

SLIGO CREEK PUBLISHING
SILVER SPRING, MD 20901
www.sligocreekpublishing.com

BEARING WITNESS
POEMS FOR TROUBLED TIMES

Edited by

ALAN ABRAMS

and

JENNIFER POLHEMUS

Awards Jury

MARK INGEBRETSEN
JOHN ROCHE
RICHARD PEABODY

FIRST PRIZE

"Early Elegy to Myself"
by
Casey Zella Andrews

SECOND PRIZE

"Instagram Censored Genocide"
BY
HIBBAH JARMAKANI

THIRD PRIZE

"Refugee"
BY
DANIEL SKATCH-MILLS

HONORABLE MENTION

"Fighting Through Tough Soil"
BY
KATHY PON

I am History,
with my frayed, damp cuffs,
my undimmed eye, my lonesome teeth.
And I will wait here by your door,
with my broken songs, unfinished,
waiting only to be written down.

~ Luther Jett, *"¡No Pasarân!"*

TABLE OF CONTENTS

INTRODUCTION

"O, I have suffered
With those that I saw suffer…"
 ~ *The Tempest,* Act I Scene 2

What does it mean to "bear witness?" To bear witness, we do
three things - become fully present, listen without judgment, and
reflect with clarity.

But this does not mean the poems in this collection are uncritical.
What separates them from some purely journalistic exercise is the
element of empathy. These poems hear the cries that echo in their
imagery. They taste the bitterness of someone else's meal.

At the same time, they are poems, which means that use all the
sensual tools that turns words into music—rhyme and rhythm,
and a host of devices that elevate bare facts into a higher kind of
truth—a truth the heart knows best.

 ~ *The Editors*

RW Mayer
No Kings

So, Tillie. When people ask you how old you were
when you went to your first
protest demonstration—what will you tell them?
You could say that you were in the neighborhood
of 300 days old. You might also tell them
that your mother MADE you go.
Stuffed you into her backpack like a Hoagie sandwich.

But then, you seemed to like it. Your Grandpa made faces
at you to make you smile. And it worked.
Perhaps you enjoyed riding around on your mother's back
listening to all the voices and seeing so many colorful signs.
You probably wished you could walk better than you did then,
because that green grass on the huge field looked quite inviting.

You were one of thousands in this town, millions across the nation,
showing up to say that we will not accept what is being done.
We are a melting pot of many different flavors
who care about each other
and stand for a democracy that represents the people.

It's not anger that moves us, though there is some of that.
No, it's primarily a love of our neighbors, our fellow citizens,
our school mates,
our recent arrivals. We stand to say we are together.

Our democracy deserves protection and we defend it.
You were there, Tillie.
We'll tell you more about it
and show you pictures when
you're older.

We were Millions.

RW MAYER
PRAYER FOR MYSELF

because that is their nature.
Don't let yourself get upset
it's just the way they are
you can't change it.

they are corrupt because
that is just the way they are,
greedy because that is
who they are

no use getting
your skivvies into a bunch
about it

there is too much to
do today
to squander energy on
judgements

clothes to wash
food to chop and peel
books to read and
contemplate
someone to help with
a struggle they have
music to make,
and listen to—

whatever happens
it simply is.
Still, there are things that need doing.

CAROL J. SCAMMAN
GOLDEN AGE GULAG

Should I bolt, buy me a gun, bug out and flee?
Before Alligator Alcatraz swallows me?
Could the gator guards arrange an *accident*,
Or I die of thirst as storms lash the locked tents?
Would sweat drown me on Native's patrimony?
Would my blood toast mosquitoes' matrimony?
Should I give searing desert sands a hot kiss,
If I'm shackled by grasping arms in Fort Bliss?
Should I run to the new Canadian state,
Or be banished by the gulag's clanging gate?

PETER GREGG SLATER

THINGS THAT GO TRUMP IN THE NIGHT

Trump bumps in the dark
throwing us off our mark.

12:30 am: Executive Order
erasing Canadian border.

1:27 am: Rant on X
blasting illegal Mex.

1:43 am: Text to the richest man:
for MAGA donation of 800 grand.

2:56 am: Beautiful tariff
on the Welsh city, Cardiff.

3:12 am: Bro note to Putin
for whom still rooting.

3:47 am: Truth Social on DEI
wishing this EVIL to die.

4:22 am: Call to JD Vance
disparaging terrible France.

All night: Ching, ching, ching
from the non-stop global grifting.

Trump bumps in the dark
leaving their nasty mark.

Sharon Scholl

INAUGURATION POEM

We stand today in a riot's wreckage
on steps carved by slave labor
on land stolen from its residents.

We pledge allegiance to a constitution
written by the time's best minds
for a people who despise intelligence.

We provide freedom to seek truth
to people who believe lies and demand
a fraudulent vote to make America great.

We provide police protection for those
who prefer mob rule, the right to own guns
to those who deny restraint by laws.

We guarantee the exercise of power
in pursuit of their ideals to many
who deny those rights to everyone else.

JOAN HARVEY
TECOLUCA EL SAVADOR USA

What are they lying down for us
A thousand bodies of shaved heads
Symmetry.
The heads the bare dark heads
Identical
To unknowing eyes
A repeating
The cold floors the cold cement
The cold.
Endure or cure
A theater of strongman illusion
Illustration of narcissistic aggression
Tornado winds in the
Whirlpool of echos
Our voices barely
Return, even to us.

We are warm here warm
We who still have hair and haircuts
That we ourselves have chosen
We who still choose what clothes to wear
While each day we watch
Elevation of pathology of mediocrity
Of sadism of incompetency
Masking as potency
Shallow facade concealing
The shallow underpinning
Of empty lives.

Look at the photos
Bare bodies packed together
Bare bodies packed with no space between
Photos of bodies just below the advertisement for expensive perfume
Photos of bodies just above the advertisement for elegant shirts
Permanent exile permanent punishment

Permanent confinement
Brutal whim brutal fear brutal beatings
A death cult we do not mourn.
Exterminating, encircling
A stutter of suffering
Reposition the bodies
Into captive shapes.

Each day cruelty each day dread
Each day confusion each day confession
Each day skin each day tongue
Each day pathology each day edicts
Each day sorrow each day drones.

A woman with inflated lips
A woman with inflated breasts
Poses in front of symmetrical bodies
How sexy she is with her $50,000 watch
How sexy she is with her gun
How sexy she is with her cruelty
How sexy she is
In in her contract with death.

Rip away the future
Rip away the history
Rip away the choice
Of how to live.
Throw away
That battered idea
Of justice
We want one voice
To lead us
To embody us
His desires are our desires
These golden rooms we meet in
These golden toilets we shit in
These golden planes we fly in
This marching music these lethal guns.

We a Christian nation
Cleanse the society
Of its vermin.
We love our white baby breeders
We love our intoxicated autocrats
We a Christian nation
Find a rapist to lead us
We a Christian nation
Love our white racists
Love our white murderers
Love our white thugs.

No sunlight no visitors
No lawyers no privacy
No phone calls
No mattresses no books
No forks no knives no spoons
No prospect ever
Of release.

Where is the border
Of this land this economy
Edges, liminal
This flesh these cries
This spinning world
This evening drifting
Into blackest night.

Outsource
Our torture
Our brutal impulses
Each day cruelty
Each day dread.
We look at the photos
We grow more cautious
We talk
Just a little bit
Less.

A CALL TO YIELD

Wrath, sharp and jagged.
Manifested as arrows, launched by an adversary, Crashes into me with
brute force.
Father, is that you?
Hot air rushes out of his mouth.
And acts as a conduit for his searing remarks.
He is a dragon;
Flame spitting, fierce, fire-blooded.
Blood that is split on cold porcelain.
He is wounded.
Mother is that you?
Clutching the bow, assuming an archer's stance.
She too is scalding, and battle ready
A volcano erupting. She shoots lava from her mouth, And it burns my
soles. They are hands, and feet. They are Tugging, striking, banging.
I am begging them to yield.
Stop. Stop. Stop.
My cries ascend and dissipate.
I am a vinyl trapped in a loop.
Their panting functions as music.
Fast, heavy, rhythmic.
My heart serves as a drum.
Boom Boom Boom.
Please stop.
Determination has etched itself on their faces.
One of them must win, Else the battle was for naught.
There is no resolution, Only a resolute winner. A victor.
Hands flailing. Feet thudding. Words.
Bitter words. Trenchant words.
They pierce and tear.
Yet they return for more.
Sadistic masochists; they must continue.
Blood and bone. I am afraid.
For myself. For them.
For only the dead have seen the end of war.

JUDITH P. OPPENHEIM

2021, SUMMER OF RAGE

I. He's fifteen.
His mother's boyfriend
Crushed his jaw and
Killed his kid-brother, Ken.
His apartment hot
It smells like rot
With bugs on floors, doors, and stairwells.
He is scared of the dark
And cries out
When roaches chew Ken's face
Angel of Death sockets stare through him
Around walls, overhead spying
Peeling paint on the ceiling.
He piles blankets over the corpse
And runs-for-his-life to hang at the park
Where he falls asleep in the sandbox
To live, late-night music at Astroworld, nearby.

II. He's a fish
That dives and flies
Under fences, over turnstiles
Through a current of heads and hands.
He surges to the stage,
Lifted by waves that bob then faint,
Like ropes of tired meat
From a grinder
I can't breathe,
He lip-syncs on shoulders
Of those in panic.
Fans fall execution-style,
Taken down by a choke-hold
From a beast with one-thousand knees.
I'm an angel,
He flies free with the fireworks.
Phones, shoes, vomit
rain against his rise.

III. Shouts bark
fists pump
red trucks race.
Parked cars
speed-chase,
skateboards beat.
Crowds spread
like blood
on a bandage
sirens blare
like speakers
on a rampage.
Recoup Reload Retweet Bend-a-Knee
No Justice, No Peace
Marchers cry
No piece, No Justice
Caps and guns reply
Hurry worry eviction die.

-CODA-
Summer burns out.
Fall floods in.
Abandoned. angry.
Restless. forlorn.
The people cannot rest
In peace
anytime. anyplace. anyway. anymore.

HANNAN KHAN

UNWARRANTED

Black helmets with dark masks,
Rope him, bag him, tag him like a rodeo calf.
Check him off their flawed list.

Trailer-plopped, zipped and tossed, he is stiff, in shock.
In the cold hold of a military plane,
Destination, El Salvador.

Judge's orders ignored, he is jailed.
Threatened by the gang that chased him
To asylum court years ago.

Like bareback bull riding, thrown back-and-forth,
His protective status argued before judges,
SCOTUS rules in his favor, his return secured.

Cowboy Clown fires attorney who spoke to the press,
Doc DOJ makes excuses,
Then, delay after delay.

But contest not over 'til the fat coyote sings;
Newfound charges steered 'round the ring:
A piece of half-cocked, bucked-up tobacco covered in spit.

He lands in Tennessee, another trial, another ruling,
Another stay and flight, to another detention
Best-of-Show-Country, Uganda.

Just like they ran that January 6 day, Congress flies the coup,
I am outraged but not surprised.
The writing was all over the cow pen walls.

Amidst the dirt, clay, sweat, and sand,
Another unwarranted deportation,
Another set of rights bites the trail.

ALLISON CARB SUSSMAN

ROCKET ATTACK

She sees the photo in the newspaper, the ruins of a playground,
a shattered house—

Noon, and a rocket crashes through the front door,
slams through room after room,
stops short of the blue-eyed girls' bedroom.

The twin sisters flatten their hips against a remaining wall,
hold slippery hands.

One sister smells like wet earth,
the other like bitter milk.

Stars and sunlight waltz through the living room.

Dazedly, their father clutches a book,
uprights a jagged shelf.

The mother rocks the baby in her arms, weeps.

The twins watch specks of dirt settle like flies on broken floor tiles,
listen to the ballooning silence---

She lets the news clipping fall, unable to speak.

ALISON CARB SUSSMAN

BLOCKADE

At night roadblocks sprang up through the Galilee.
Soldiers appeared with big army vehicles, Uzis, flashlights.
The moon hovered above us.
Close air sifted through our little truck.
One warrior, almost as young as me,
but with dark circles under his eyes,
stuck out his hand for our driver's ID.
Benny handed it over.
I fiddled with the radio dial to get the army station,
so the fighter would think we were "A-Okay."
The other volunteers, also seventeen,
lay in the back of the truck, asleep.
Benny was twenty, responsible for us.
What if the soldier wouldn't let him pass?
What if he caught me with secret codes up my shirt?
The conscript flipped through Benny's documents.
Minutes ticked away on my wristwatch.
A smile across his mouth, the combatant
handed Benny back his papers
and waved us through.

JULIANA SCHIFFERES

STATISTICAL INSIGNIFICANCE

Politics is a game of probabilities.
Voters may attack causes
with self-interest and self-understanding
other times we stab
at phantoms.

Am I small, a data point?
I tremble before my negligibility.
Where is the individual
enshrined within our founding documents?
Is democracy a game of mathematics
blind to our rage and hope?

Is each difference between us simply a margin of error,
is each misrecognition a confound?
Neighbors are strangers behind the curtain of the voting booth.
What is lost in consultants' calculus?

We are turf-cut, we become our zip codes
as canvassers and campaigns interrogate
Pavlovian slogans, well-trained rage:
are we really a nation of community, or are we one of NextDoor?

COOPER SMITH
2.5 HOURS TO LEE'S FERRY VIA FLAGSTAFF

6 stars of the
Seven sisters, last
One lost to memory
And light faded from a sky
No Longer ours

5 hours round
Trip from Flagstaff
To sit beside the muzzled
Mouth of a river, muffled
But not yet mute

4 Wild Horses
Gaunt as harbingers.
Riderless, bony spines
Bearing hell, having shed
The burden of man

3, the trinity
Laid bare, naked
As water works upon
The broken stone
Under unyielding sky

2 sides to
A barb wire fence
Whether stretched between
Grazing land or genocide marks,
Have and have not

1 thread tying
Us all to the bounty
Or bankruptcy of life
Carried on the back
Of a river

0 the openness
Of decisions not yet
Made, make a promise
To act before the clock
Hits zero

COOPER SMITH

GILDED AGE

"Only in America"
Crackling out of the radio
Tires retracing imaginary lines
Between borders and belonging
Of a landscape transected.
Traveling across the tracks
Of a border patrol
Side quest

Vultures of the void
Searching for Skeletons,
Sending bones back to
Point of origin. As the
Dry mouth desert
Stands questioning

When will the rain come?

Saguaros stand stoically
Arms outstretched, awaiting
The sweeping sheets of
Soft winter showers
That are yet withheld.
Holding dry dust under
Cracked fingernails, I am
Digging for answers
Under desert pavement

Knuckles bleeding
Into bedrock, manos
Of my own flesh, mix
With mesquite to
Grind meal
From my bones

The same empty basins
Sitting like asking hands
As the bighorn succumb,
Sunken into sleepless
Dreams of drought.

Empty tinajas, metates
ground until they have
Nothing left to give
Tracing lines of patina
Paint receding rings
Of falling water level,
A dividing line between
Perishing and plenty.

Hollow eyes looking
Toward the glowing
Golden hills of the
Cholla, a gilded land
Of withered leaves

Decadence adorning Drought

Only in America
Will we peer from
The pyre of our own
Demise and praise
The impending glow.
Only in America will
We mistake it's opulence
For the dawning of
A golden age.

KATERINA MUSIENKO

GRAMMAR EXERCISE

The swan's neck of a question mark
is the only thing you need
to form a question in my native tongue.
In English, you let the building blocks of a sentence
fall apart
to rearrange them into a single act of interrogation.
The pure mechanics, the physics, the logic of this exercise,
the magnetic pull of a question word plus auxiliary plus the dance of
subjects, objects and verbs on the string of tight-fitting beads—
language string theory—brings me joy.
The numbness to the meaning that comes with it,
detaching form from truth
is disturbingly invigorating, empowering, god-like.

Watch:
"43 piffity clobs crampupled a spludge in the clouds."
How many clobs? What did they crampuple? Was piffity their size or
taste?
A nonsensical language output that makes complete grammatical sense.

One of these days
on my way home from work
a statement assaulted
the peaceful hum of my mind.
Allow me to dissect it until I
reach the realm of blissful numbness.

"There is a war in my home country."
Is there a war in my home country?
Where is the war?
What is there in my home country?
Has there always been/will there always be?
Whose home country is the war in?
What is war?
What is home?
When was the airport shut down—

look, here comes the passive voice—
in my hometown due to, because of or thanks to the war?
When will I/will I ever be able
to show my six-year-old the city his parents grew up in,
met in, argued, made up and married in?
Will he be seven or eight or nine
when he crosses that border
for the very first time
since leaving at the age of one
holding no memory beyond the universe of his mom.
Was it worth it then?
Is it worth it now?
Will it ever be worth it
to miss seeing my sister pregnant?
Never putting my hand on her belly?
Never seeing my niece as a baby and smelling that spot on her neck?
Is it worth it to cry at a hint of a chance
that I might never see my grandpa again. Alive. Before the end.

Will it be worth it in the end
to know how to write this in English,
having allowed its thumps, stomps and rhythms
to replace the swan song of my native tongue?
When is the end?

There is a war in my home country.
Will I ever be truly back?

Ian Hall

Love in the Time of Company Towns

Nothing worth nothing ever happens
after midnight. Coroners & dairy

farmers alike have told me this, & you should believe
every atom of it. But, then again, a godgiven rule

is humbled by its exception. Tonight, for instance, I am
inevitable. You & me, your curls tasseling out

like a 4-H project, are hoofing pell-mell
down the mountainside to the birthing hips

of the Big Sandy, hallooing *there is no such joy
in the pharmacy as on the road thereto.* Boneheads

to the letter of the law. Eyes amok with dilation, I want the deed
to the way this swimming hole looks just now—all bluing

& moonburnt. Vague twang of chum. The cattail
astir like tooth-torn garters. Usually, I'm too gummed up

in everydayness to appreciate this
claptrap idyll. But right this second I need no convincing

that both my feet are planted angelic in the heartland
of the real. With ring fingers you fishhook

my nose. *Get a royal whiff of that,* you say, & I mainline
the menstrual zest of a river in July. Lo-Fi

sublime. Water busks over the bosom of stones. Lusty
crickets won't take maybe for an answer. Tomorrow surely

there'll be another frog-strangling rain. Too spongey to ply
a trade, earn a troglodyte living, roofers & loggers might

mass here to fish, drink, lie, swap
lore. Might connive against their foremen, some

litigious homeowner. & I too will be out
another day's greenback roughage. But this doesn't peeve—

I can always binge
you through the billable hours. *Thwack.* I just went to palm

one of your glands petite, but the drowsy piles of rock
we were idling against made a tattletale sound & with malice

came apart. We are side-by-side on the grass now, sides
splitting. *Chalk a line around us as we lay, & this'd be right*

tragic. More star-crossed than Heloise & Abelard. Still airy
& elfin from the vertigo, you ask if those are the names

of the teacher & student who got caught holding pagan
angles in the supply closet at the vocational school? *More*

or less, I say, & course my hand up your spine
like a Geiger counter—pausing above the pastoral

inflections, the haute scoliosis, to *bleep* animatronic. Grinning,
our fingers duet. We are close enough to know each other

biblically. So close I can hear the gristle
creak in your back when you move

your mouth to mine. Now we are not talking
swine futures or the Technicolor horrors that haunt

the CSPAN ticker. There is noise, but not a trifle of that. What home
steads between us: sighs, yips, small gallantries, air

sacs daubed in ancestral gunk. Right now, there's strictly this
Strepthroat patter—hot, thoughtless. Like a gamboling lamb, you go

to & fro. The flats of my feet sizzle
with hookworm.

LESLIE YOUNGE

UPON RETURNING HOME FROM EXILE

When the fog lifted, the fruit trees, though blackened and bruised,
were still erect among the rubble, and hope glimmered like a floater
briefly blurring months of destruction and displacement.

Then the shadows moved and we saw clearly the crumble:
through a gaping hole the staircase pendulous, a rebar chandelier,
no windows and no doors, the vines swallowing bricks like snakes.

Seeing life would be built from scratch we made bread
to practice believing that water, flour, yeast, salt, and oil
still alchemize into sustenance, phoenix rising from ash.

LESLIE YOUNGE

TOMORROW, TOMORROW AND TOMORROW

After Deborah Roberts, 2023

Every Deborah Roberts collage
of a little Black boy surrenders
to his face, his hands, his stare.
Not Ralph Yarl age 16,
but my boy, age 9, knocking on a door
answered by a gun.
Each tomorrow is under fire
as it dares approach the horizon.
Our sons have been turned into soldiers,
fighting only for the dawn.
The stolen days have cost the most.
The tomorrows with plans
for play and for hard work,
for rest and for loving and for living.
It's the tomorrows we want back,
emptied of fear, emptied of pain, emptied of grief.
The tomorrows are the only real reparation.
Give us what we are owed.

JOAN WHITE

GOOD JOURNALISM TELLS US WHO, WHAT, WHEN, WHERE, AND WHY

Fool's spring. Sugar snow melts as it hits the ground. Flood watch. The river below the house swells, breaches. Wipes out the beaver dam. I stand on the bank waiting. For what? To see how they rebuild. Their inner life so simple — The dam. The lodge. Is this what makes courage possible? Out west biologists copy them, creating dams of mud and leaves and branches. To restore the floodplains. To hold back the wildfires. Quiet ways to save the burning world. But our orders were to *make some noise…some good trouble.* A student speaks to hold back the missiles firing. Who was detained? The hallowed halls recede into the shadows. Radio Static. Voice of America furloughed. Chilled speech. Guts of social security spill onto the rose garden lawn. Reading only the headlines, I cut the news accounts short like a guillotine. Big Bird accused of driving the federal deficit. Someone screams at Elmo, "Are you a globalist?" When Dorothy threw a bucket of water to save the scarecrow from the fire, the sodden witch cried, *I'm melting! Melting!* Dorothy claimed it was an accident. Down by the river, felled sumac and dogwood and birch. Beaver totems with pointed heads. A rusted sign post no longer a sign post. A red mitten hangs on it.

M. JEANETTE KELLEHER

THE WISSAHICKON

Forbidden Drive's gravel path is mostly vacant
the sparse few travelers holding
hats to heads and coats to chests against the April gale.

I like the park this way.
The sycamores mine and the split rail fence
keeping me apart from the creek
while I run the rocky runnels. A moment away
From the gangrenous divorce.

Three boys ahead, teenagers
Arm in arm, *how sweet*, I think
as they embrace against the bracing wind.

But then the veil lifts:
Like a dream sequence
Where the house around you crumbles
and you fall from a cliff
startled awake.

The hand at the back clarifies into a pistol:
a flower turned spider.
The realization prickles through my armpits
and makes my legs unsolid.

These boys aren't skipping
but walking the boy in between them
pressure from both sides to keep him in line
a gun pressed hard in his back,
the gun stark against
the boy's white hoodie.

This is an execution.

All I see is my son.
If this were my son
who would care for my son?

I run unsure of my task but sure of feet
and when I break the trees
call the police.
The next day my back seizes up
and I can't lift my son.

Three days later a body bobs up
where the Wissahickon meets the Schuylkill.
On the neighborhood page people complain
that the first responder presence chokes traffic
and someone posts a photo of a body
under a blue tarp
from a distance fuzzy behind the rails
that block the falls near the bus stop–
someone's son.

KEITH DAVID PARSONS
WERTH

It has been twenty-four years
since I saw the second plane hit.
I was nineteen and in college;
have now lived most of my life
in the shadow of that day.

Anton Bruce was also nineteen
when the round came for him,
four years now, in Afghanistan
he was liked, even loved
the squad called him "Werth"

after his favorite ball player
who he resembled
in a pre-boot-camp pic.
He was born, lived, and died
in the shadow of our grief,

and rage, and decisions.
I blame him for joining
or perhaps Osama bin Laden
also dead, a decade now.
They say don't blame the victim

as if we cannot mutually
victimize each other,
as if death were
mutually exclusive.
Our justice is full

of such justifications
every bullet
leaving Werth's gun
every drop of blood
leaving his body.

We demand them;
to do otherwise would
be to participate whole-
heartedly in these killings,
let our intent make us murderers.

Instead we treat an
incomprehensible tragedy
as an excuse: when they go low
we fall down a rabbit hole
of hubris; drag Werth with us.

Did he believe as he bled
he was advancing a cause?
Did he cling to that light
as his eyes darkened?
Or did he doubt,

as I do,
never the value
of his sacrifice
but if it was
worth it.

RODRIGO TOSCANO

CHARMS

It's a charmed life—when your pets are healthy
Charm knocked on a charmed door, looking for charm
When children on your street are running free
Charm was greeted by charm, and welcomed in
When old people are well taken care of
Charm was offered honey chocolate babkas
When your home is secure, and can live there
Charm reached into its bag, offering dates
When your neighbor's not sick with avarice
Charm was immensely charmed by the exchange
When barbed wire walls aren't the grim master
Charm thanked charm again, and moseyed on home
When you've a million friends you've never met
Charm slipped into bed and slept peacefully

KEITH DAVID PARSONS
BAIL

One look and the storm comes back
pounding rain, roar of a river errant
the bloated creak of miles
of hills and bottomland under
god knows how many gallons
oak tops barely cresting like mangroves.

The strive to survive, save
the day the water rose and you dug
down deep, muscles aching from
clutching the oar like a hatred
the frail canoe's ruddy cheeks
holding the children like a breath.

It has been five hundred six days
you can't feel them but
know the date and can head-count
don't remember seeing the canoe since
don't know why one of your
empties bobs in the water
reaching to the gunwale.

You drain your bottle and bend
weary oar on the currents of now.
Now the water fills the canoe's mouth.
Now the storm is inside.

EMILY ARUNA TEITSWORTH

MAYRA

I. Concepción

"Loca," they told her, "you're even crazier than your mother." No one
admitted that it was the idea you get when you're all out of ideas – not

uncommon among them. Mother, grandfather, baby sister – people as
chains by weight, not metaphor: the price of infant formula, blood

pressure medicine, firewood. Endless hours standing behind the pharmacy
counter, watching a line of Tabcin packets flutter in the

breeze. The days compressed like sediment, burying themselves together,
deep in the earth. In December her courage waned with the light. Then

the new year arrived and like that the tinny fireworks set off the idea
again to rattle in her skull. *Al norte.* The second Tuesday in March she

didn't intend anything but then her mother's flattened stare, the
neighbor spitting on their stoop as he passed, same as every morning.

She knew there was a land somewhere out beyond exhausted and ashamed.
And so she just started walking towards it, walking away.

II. Trail

While she rested the path spooled out in brilliant neon, always shimmering
up ahead – a little farther, barely out of reach. When

she rose she had to remind herself, there is no trail. No line on a
map, only trains, hunger, dogs huddled in ditches, and so much dust.

Everyone else had someone and she had only herself. She knew her
family was desperate for her and so for weeks she sang to them as

she walked. The days grew hotter, swelling and compressing, sand
and sweat. Suddenly she was part of the scattered masses coalescing

against the fence. The coyotes circled, buzzards without wings,
desperate men. She knew they could smell her fear like a rotting

animal, incubating in this place sworn to the mission of going
anywhere better. She had always been faithful to God. She knew she

could heal with her hands. She could sew. "There is more for me in
this world," she murmured, as she ducked under the barbed wire.

III. Cadavers

The man slept silently all night, slumped back into a bush. She didn't
want to wake him but water was moving through her mind in rivers,

drying her tongue against her teeth. "*Señor…*" She reached out, shook
him, felt the sickening lightness of his arm under the jacket. The sky

shuddered against a far line of mountains, hair framed the man's skinless
face. He was missing a foot. She fell back but the burning in her throat

insisted. A bottle of water, dry crackers from his pack. She finished
them all and got up slowly, like a stunned rabbit. She was still lost,

alive in a desert made of bones. Her prayers rose into the ruthless blue and
cracked against the ceiling of the world. She wandered, for how

many hours, maybe days, until they caught her. Men who looked like
people she knew, who pushed her through one door after another,

who shoved her finally into a cave of phantoms, the dead eye of a
storm, a concrete arroyo in the winterscape of her dreams.

IV. Ghost

Dark, saturated dawn, before sunlight broke against the narrow window.
Too early for lawyers or guards. She felt her first, then saw the girl

standing alone in the corner of her cell, crying as if she had just
learned she was a ghost. *Yo soy tu otra tu.* A taste of iron in her

throat, her wish rising like a bird made of smoke: to take one of
those small hands in hers, to walk out the door towards an

imagined destiny, that universe of corn kernels and money and
fire. "I fell," whispered the ghost, "like you." We rise where we

stand, wherever our feet touch earth. So many miles to get to this
nowhere at the center of everything. The judge muttered his official

curse, sentenced her for standing on the wrong land, proclaimed
the end of her story the same as the beginning. She knew that

could never be true and so she told him the simple facts:
"My name is Mayra, I am 17 years old. I am your other you."

V. Light

Ten thousand points of light, blinking, extinguished, stuttering back
to life. Morse code narrating this brutal randomness, the light

following our steps, this crush of light bursting within us,
the light illuminating a path that disappears ahead as we walk.

Mayra was born in the summer, in a town where girls drank fertilizer
and slept forever. The future was heavy as stone, white as ash.

She carried the cardinal directions burning with delirium in her heart,
a wild resolution to shine, to dazzle. Her footsteps made a trail

along the spine of the continent, holding the earth together like stitches
on a wound. Whether she made it home is not the question.

The birds, the ghosts, the mountains still sing a song
that sounds like her voice, a wind carrying sparks to light the next fire.

Emily Aruna Teitsworth
End Times Cookbook

We call on the goddesses to help us,
now that there's no one else.
Craters replace children, cactus grow
instead of olive trees. The journalists
have all filed their last story and disappeared.

We are done justifying our lives,
the fact that we cost more than nothing, too.
Today I'd like to thank Yemaya for the gentle force
of the tides. I'll bow to Hecate and keep walking.
Take one more sip from Meng Po's bowl.

But for the end times, only Kali will do.
Someone who isn't afraid to trample
on the gods, to carry a severed head
like a purse, to breathe rot into the air
and pant like a wolf.

The wind today is blowing towards the innocent,
the hopeful, the rambling, and the old.
Sparks trace the breeze. Kali arrived
just in time to burn everything down,
arranged her charcoal-washed limbs
among the ashes, polished her silver trident.
From far away, even the bombs look beautiful.

We line up for our turn in her 10-armed embrace,
returning our pain to the flesh of the goddess.
This is how I'd like to end, suffocated by love
and protection, our creator scaling away evil
as easily as scouring a pot, ready to teach us
how to cook something new, a bone broth
to sustain us as we march to the next world.

JULIA LISELLA

BOSTON COMMON

Boston Common was just the way I want to feel
weed smoke wafting its gentle skunk scent.
We spied some shade away from the homeless guys
and risked that the cool air was temporary, just a passing cloud.
I pressed the small of my back to the dirty bench as we talked
mother and son, though we could be friends today as I forgot myself
and just said the next things, and those next things friends talk about.
The park was full of noisy men
really laughing
like in a good country
but not really; I don't know now what country
can grow here or why the heart
gets trained to shrink. *Their hearts are so small* you said
about the angry customers who come to your restaurant.
I didn't want to leave you and yet couldn't believe
it was really not so hard. *Walk me to the station steps* I said
and you walked me there, my hug shaking your whole body
from right to left like my love could take you
just about anywhere.

Julia Lisella

Psalm for Roe v. Wade

I am God's body in the world,

I share in the breath of the trees
these are God's arms, these are his legs,

but you there believe you are God's body,
arms grown to push me

legs grown to block my way. God,
I thought you did not believe in war

but you created it. Holy is the hell between us,
holy is the road they claim, holy is the violence

made all night by God's body in the world.
I sleep fitfully, cry out where my body is tonight?

God, you're a stranger to me now
when men in the world can claim you.

I wear my quiet shoes, walk in the dark,
feel my way into the houses of friends.

All day we have been singing
and weeping beside the riverbank

lay down your grievances against the women of your lives, our power

LESLEY YOUNGE

THE TIMES

After Lucille Clifton

We are trying to understand these times, these
days of war when so many sobbing beings are saying remember my child
    too.
We wonder about those who drop bombs and hold guns and are
trying to protect their children with war so we ask are your
children worth the trigger pull, are the bullets flying worth your children,
Are your children worth the high you get off conquest because this
is not the way towards peace, which would save your children too.
Why not lift our arms to create instead of destroy? What is
life after we have buried such precious detritus, once not your
child wrapped in cloth and lowered into the earth, now too your child?

TARA W. ZAFFT

THE VIOLIN CRIES

She plays the violin while we lie on yoga mates. Proud
I am here. Not at home, waiting for sirens. But I
need to be away from the fear of my walls. And calls
from mothers and children and friends. Afraid. For
us. We lie and feel the breeze. From the sea. Her strings
transport me to another time. I begin to see Shabbat candles
Shabbat candles on tables. White linen tablecloths. Worn
from wars. And pogroms. This is not the first time we have
feared. Fought. Survived. The Shabbat candles burn. The
violin cries.

Translated from the original Russian by
TONY BRINKLEY & RAINA KOSTOVA

LINES ON THE UNKNOWN SOLDIER
by Osip Mandelshtam

1

Let this air be witness -
to his heartbeat battling in the distance -
and omnivorous, toxic in the trenches
is an ocean, mass without an opening.

Why should stars be so abusive:
why should they see everything - to eye
and sentence judge and witness to an ocean,
mass without a window?

The unkind farmer, rain recalls,
his nameless manna,
how a wood of crosses marked
an ocean or a battle's wedge.

Cold and ailing, men
will murder, cold and starved,
and in his well-marked grave
we place an unknown soldier.

Ailing swallow, teach me if you will,
you who are forgetting how to fly,
how to steer without a sail or wing,
but with a grave above me in the sky.

And for Mikhail Lermontov
I give a rigorous account,
how the stooped learn from the grave,
and how the aerial pit attracts.

2

Like grapes that stir and rustle,
these communities of worlds alarm us,
and the tents of outstretched constellations -
oils of golden constellations - tensile clusters -
hover over us like stolen cities,
gossip, gilded slips of tongue,
berries of toxic cold . . .

3

Through an ether decimally labelled
the light-world of velocities, ground to a beam,
starts the count, translucent
with the radiant pain and mole of zeroes.

But triangular, crane-like, across a field of fields
a new field flies -
news flies along a path of glowing dust,
a battle radiates from yesterday.

The news flies on a path of glowing dust -
I am not Leipzig, I am not Waterloo,
and I am not a Battle of the Nations. I - the new -
from me comes light to light.

Marbled-black, an oyster's deep recess
in which the light of Austerlitz dies out -
the Mediterranean swallow squints,
the plague-infested sand of Egypt sticks.

4

An Arabian medley, muddled, tangled, crumbling,
world-light of velocities, ground to a beam -
on my retina the beam pauses
in my eye on squinted feet.

Millions of dead men cheaply killed
have walked a path through emptiness -
good night! best wishes to them all!
from the facade, the face of these earth-fortresses.

Sky of the trenches, incorruptible,
the sky of mass, of wholesale deaths,
beyond, behind - away from you - entirely -
I am moving with my lips in darkness.

Beyond the craters, behind embankments,
scree - where he lingered, darkened, overturning -
gloomy, pockmarked, the unsettled graves'
             belittled genius.

5

Foot soldiers die nicely,
the night choir crows nicely
over Schweik's flattened smile,
above the poultry-lance of Don Quixote,
over the bird-knight's metatarsus.
The cripple befriends the human:
both will find employment.
And tapping at the margins of the century's eyelids -
families of wooden crutches chattering -
friendship, comrades! - the earth's orb!

6

Is it for this the skull unfolds -
from temple to temple - the entire span:
that armies, their soldiers, will flow only
through the precious sockets of his eyes?
The skull unfolds from living -
the entire span - temple to temple -
teasing itself with a purity of stitches,
refining itself as a cupola of insight,
foaming with thinking, dreaming itself itself -
the cup of cups and fatherland of fatherlands -
its cap embroidered with an astral rib -
good fortune's cap of happiness and blessings -
      Shakespeare's father.

7

The ash-tree's clarity, the sycamore's vigilance,
reddening barely, speed toward home -
as if they were casting spasms of magic,
addressing each heaven with its dull fires.

What allies us, only the superfluous,
before us - not the failure, but an error
in the measure - with no model - and the air,
      enough to breathe, to fight
for air is glory that is unlike any other.

Is magic packed and stored
in voids of empty space for this,
that white stars, racing backward,
barely reddening, speed toward home?

And casting on my consciousness, half-spasmed
being - without option -
whether I drink this potion,
whether it is my head that I am eating under fire?

Night - stepmother of the star's encampment -
Do you sense what is to be?

8

Blood swells the aortas
and the rows resound in a whisper:
I was born in '94,
I was born in '92 . . .
And, squeezing in my fist) - clutching the used year -
        the worn-out year of my birth - herding
with the crowd as one,
with my bloodless mouth I whisper:
I was born on the night of the second and third
of January, in '91 - the ninety-first,
a year without hope - and centuries
encircle me with fire.

2 March 1937-1938

SARAH E. DAS GUTPA

SEEMA SPEAKS

"I am part of an Indian army, an invisible army,
a hidden force, an underground battalion,
an army of twenty million women construction workers.
I have stolen a few minutes from mixing cement
to have a few words with you. A few minutes away from the heat,
the dust, the pollution, the worry about my daughter
back in the village with my parents.
Today I'm helping Mona, her baby's due next week,
she's finding it hard to carry the bricks, she's dizzy
and I'm scared she might fall.
Of course, we can't earn more, we can't be trained
for the skilled work of men.
 I know I could do it.
I could cut wood or lay bricks.
I carved a doll out of an old scrap of wood.
The face was soft and delicate, the eyes were laughing too.
My daughter played with it, instead of sitting,
crawling in the dust and rubble.
Soon I have to break up stones. They're often too hot to touch,
don't look at my hands, they are rougher than the bricks.
Some of the women here are strong.
They earn enough to care for their children alone.
Yes, they've left abusive husbands.
Got their kids into school.
I still dream of that.
I came back to work, the day after my son died-
just four months he was-

'I'm coming, no need to shout.'"

Andrew McClean

PLEA

Plea to a Foreign "Terrorist"
Please spare my life;
Despite the fact that my government
has subverted your elections,
has provided arms
to extirpate your people,
has "neutralized" your loved ones.
Perhaps by your mercy
I may live,
in order to convey the truth.

WILLIAM PRINDLE

THE PRESCRIPTION

for these ailments of the public soul
might be found in the mouth

of a river that runs underground.
Perhaps the whole notion of opposition

requires nothing more than the poise
of baobab trunks or county-size mycelia.

Maybe we should apologize not to
raving narcissists but to those still

whispering their erased stories beneath
our feet. It could be that our strength

in the days to come will flow from
faculties too subtle to be muzzled,

waving imperceptibly graceful wands
that infuse the raging tide with light.

DANIEL SKACH-MILLS

REFUGEE

Before anything—

before words can be poured out,
before tears can be brewed into a story—

this woman cooking on a tin-can stove
who stops to offer American reporters tea.

Awash in the bitter aftertaste of war,
it's her smile's untarnished curve,
shimmering like the well in a spoon,
that stirs and so completely disarms us.
Bearer of shattered place settings,
it is her words' seamless weave
filtering the rain of bombs into a beverage
that slakes and expands
dried leaves and tongues
between strangers.

Tonight, the news, in brief, is this—
heart steeped in the boil-over
of a thousand sorrows,
there is no saucer in our vocabulary
that will hold a cup this large.

DANIEL SKACH-MILLS

UNION SQUARE

San Francisco, California

Forgive me, Tony Bennett—
but high on a hill, hours later,
my heart's still wishing it could leave behind
these aftershocks of street people in Frisco,
this man gaping up at us, a collapsed fault line,
sleeping—we'd like to dream, and God knows how—
between a parked car and four
Chronicle newspaper boxes.

Forgive me, if my thoughts swerve
to avoid his inevitable collision
with street sweepers and dogshit.
If my memory's backtracking cable car
keeps struggling to get over
the barely breathing hill
of his chest.

How he could die lying there,

halfway to the stars,
cheek whitewall
pressed to the curb,

where wheels
that could crush him
wouldn't be
the first.

EDWARD BARANOSKY

STOWAWAY

A billion stars go spinning through the night,
Blazing high above your head.
But in you is the presence that
Will be, when all the stars are dead…
                    --Rainer Maria Rilke

Walk with me awhile
Where the veiled spindrift of sunrise
Gilds the edges of the headlands
Shrugging off the darkness
Breaking in with the surf at dawn,
As tides of pilgrims glimpse the sight
Of morning's call through mist-hushed dunes
And the last embers of the faded moon--
In the last genesis of the fossil light
A billion stars go spinning through the night.

Come sail above the cliffs
With a simple paper kite
Scrawled with a haiku to the blue,
Breaking through the mackerel sky
Drifting with flocks of seabirds.
Listen to the naked flute torn from the seabed,
The combined song of every shore wind
And foghorn calling *Leviathan*
Gathering in a summer thunderhead
Blazing high above your head.

Awake now,
You could paint another world,
But this is yours—your paint,
Or pain can't liberate or imprison,
That's the sole plein air privilege
Or burden; to draw a format,
Or accept a challenge,
To sketch a window to the sheer
Form of existence, the *Magnificat--*
But in you is the Presence, That.

Somewhere nearby you sit,
An old man with an empty canvas,
An easel leaning against the morning wind—
A half-blind, trembling artist
Holding onto the memory of light,
The elusive color of breaking whiteheads
At the mouth of a dark harbor.
The dream, and the memory, and the painting
Are all discreet, indelible when said,
And will be, when all the stars are dead.

EDWARD BARANOSKY

THE LAST SOJOURN

Paradoxically, the distance to home
And from home are not equal.
          --Hippocrates

1

You remind yourself again,
That extinction doesn't follow rarity,
But scarcity-- You manifest yourself
On the way home, trying to explain
Why you're here, or there, or nowhere.

2

The sign that says,
"Do not touch," paradoxically
Invites touch, but your reality
Measures the extent of fragility,
Of the distance between us.

3

In the beginning
Is the proof of ending,
The reflection in a mirror,
Or black ice; the echoes
Of the falls beneath *Echo Bridge*.

4

Redwing Bay was
An idea before it was a place,
An experience before
It was a memory, corroding
Into autumn colors.

5
To draw the empty space
Is less a sketch than a creation,
A discovery of the air
Between us-- a depth of field
Scorned as illusion by the false.

6
You have cared for each cherished
Heirloom, seashells in boxes, semi-precious
Stones, photos of old dogs no longer here--
Nothing matters, but *"Hi, I'm home!"*
Even if no one answers. Everything stops here.

EDWARD BARANOSKY

STOPPING BY THE SEA

The widow's walk stands empty now,
Haunted by indelible memories.

The dark absence of tears, blanketed
By a cold morning fog--

Waiting is always too long, creating
New icons of expectation.

That dawn seems sacred now when the sea is still
Holding its breath between tides.

Communities have fought wars over their nets,
Sword fishing was everyone's religion--

The dark *Caribou* against a stark white horizon,
Pose distinct in the twilight...

Listening to a *Russian* pianist perform
Rachmaninoff, the tiger by the tail--

We are all exiles from our father's land,
On a vision quest for a secret name.

There are few secrets that are natural
Until you stop by the sea.

If you are in search of *God*
You are going in the wrong direction

JUDITH P. OPPENHEIM
UNWARRANTED

Black helmets with dark masks,
Rope him, bag him, tag him like a rodeo calf.
Check him off their flawed list.

Trailer-plopped, zipped and tossed, he is stiff, in shock.
In the cold hold of a military plane,
Destination, El Salvador.

Judge's orders ignored, he is jailed.
Threatened by the gang that chased him
To asylum court years ago.

Like bareback bull riding, thrown back-and-forth,
His protective status argued before judges,
SCOTUS rules in his favor, his return secured.

Cowboy Clown fires attorney who spoke to the press,
Doc DOJ makes excuses,
Then, delay after delay.

But contest not over 'til the fat coyote sings;
Newfound charges steered 'round the ring:
A piece of half-cocked, bucked-up tobacco covered in spit.

He lands in Tennessee, another trial, another ruling,
Another stay and flight, to another detention
Best-of-Show-Country, Uganda.

Just like they ran that January 6 day, Congress flies the coup,
I am outraged but not surprised.
The writing was all over the cowpen walls.

Amidst the dirt, clay, sweat, and sand,
Another unwarranted deportation,
Another set of rights bites the trail.

HIBBAH JARMAKANI

I KILLED THE ARABIC LANGUAGE

I came to you a stranger by blood bestowed with nativity by law
Did I inhabit a foreign land or did it inhabit me
If you ask my tongue it will lament over the richness of vocabulary
that died in my throat
Ask my dreams and they will answer in the language of those
most skilled in the cadence of death
An entire existence filtered from its own consciousness
and cut off from its life force
The impurities it leaves behind are nothing but a well of loose translations

HIBBAH JARMAKANI
INSTAGRAM CENSORED GENOCIDE

I tried to show you my child's body came to me faceless,
melted away by the force of missiles.
You told me no, they all come blurred in a patchwork of pixels.
I tried to show you my whole family perished
as I felt the heat escape their flesh.
You told me this didn't appear in your feed despite hitting refresh.
I tried to show you my people were dying from wounds
that could never heal.
You told me you must have skipped past the little bubble
that said see reel.
I tried to show you we are people too, not an array of headlines.
You told me not people to you, this goes against community guidelines.
I tried to show you my lived reality was one of inconceivable violence.
You told me from behind a screen this was far too graphic for you,
could you please die in silence.
I tried,
and I tried,
to show you I was dying,
only to die a thousand more times trying

GRANT A. MOORE

PANTOUMS OF DEMENTIA

Movement I - Undulation

the seconds slowed to stop as Father passed,
when flocking sons returned to home to mourn,
then Mother's mind began to break at last
as moments shed in threads she once had worn.

when flocking sons returned to home to mourn,
recast in lensing rays of age amassed
as moments shed in threads she once had worn
the Father's sons adorned with clothes outcast.

recast in lensing rays of age amassed
a question, Mother, may I have a dance?
the Father's sons adorned with clothes outcast
an offered hand through loops of time's expanse.

a question, Mother, may I have a dance?
their Father knelt and tender took her hand,
an offered hand through loops of time's expanse,
their final words in wilting hearts expand.

their Father knelt and tender took her hand,
the seconds slowed to stop as Father passed,
their final words in wilting hearts expand,
then Mother's mind began to break at last.

Movement II - Rearrangement

remember now before the future fades,
the sutured minutes of memories held,
records replayed as grooving sound degrades,
advancing echoes, music notes dispelled.

the sutured minutes of memories held:
now twirling dance, oh younger selves, entrance
advancing echoes, music notes dispelled
through silent waltz that swells with last romance.

now twirling dance, oh younger selves, in trance
with candled spells of woven hands that grasp
through silent waltz that swells with last romance
of eyes reshaping molds, the fated clasp.

with candled spells of woven hands that grasp
relapsing moments sung by bells and crowds
of eyes, reshaping molds the fated clasp
of past refrains now sealed beneath the clouds.

relapsing moments sung by bells and crowds
concealed by crumbling walls, demented shades
of past refrains now sealed beneath these clouds
that clutter skies in swarms that stretch decades.

concealed by crumbling walls, demented shades
(remember now before the future fades)
invade the hollowed mind as scream pervades
records replayed as grooving sound degrades.

Movement III - Dissolution

remember ancillary note sentries:
the good can decay many ways.
phantom morrow's cough. in times realize
the mention there of tenant seasons.

the good candy came anyways;
all target the damaged mind in trance,
(the men shun their often antsy sons)
the flow ingrained decomposes.

altar, get the damn aged mind, entrance
memory erstwhile, foe kissing;
the flowing rain eddy composes
another ushered

memo rehearsed while focusing
an aim, wintry slight, upward ingrown
another us heard
the fading names of suns.

a name when trees light up, warding grown
remembrance, ill airy notes in trees,
the fading names of sons
fan tomorrow's coffin, time's real eyes.

GRANT A. MOORE
EULOGY

mound of the earth, the funeral pyre,
sermons of fire, infernos of oak.

burning of briars, spiraling higher,
chorus expired and softly I spoke:

nothing is left, but cinders remain,
warm to the touch, as memories fade.

look to the thrashing showers of rain,
mourn with the hissing coils arrayed.

pound for the taking, body of ash,
weight of the flame, transmuted to wind.

thundering blacks, the cymbals that crash,
scavenging clouds, vultures descend.

weep with the water, falling to feet,
honor your father, drink of his heat.

KALI LIGHTFOOT
MATH QUIZ

How does the point spread
of the football game the Raiders lose
impact the velocity at which
a Redwing boot smashes
through the screen
of a cathode ray tube television?

After a lamp is launched
from a father's right hand
and shatters against the wall
above a daughter's bowed head,
how many glass shards
will the girl retrieve? What subset
of the total will draw blood?

How many times will
library staff break policy
to allow one brown-eyed child
to take the Princeton Review's
Best Colleges home to read
until the sun comes up,
eyes gritty with dreams
of anywhere but
in this house, in this town,
in this county, in this state?

How many invisible bees
will be blamed for fists
that find their way
through the windshield
of a powder-blue Pontiac?

Extra Credit:
What is the limit, as a woman
approaches middle age,
of asking herself if her mother
might have left sooner
had there been no children
keeping her in that carpeted kitchen?

CASEY ZELLA ANDREWS
EARLY ELEGY TO MYSELF

When the uterus got so large it had
a diameter, I wondered if the baby was
lost. When the body got bigger I wondered

what is worth that moon-ness? When the
door locks you might think
I clutch only my
own stomach? When the gun went off
you might

picture your own kid under the desk? When you
have imagined the deaths enough

it stops being
a drill. The first one I ever heard of on a small screen
gray with accusation. The protocols get longer,
longer, each a list made into an acronym made into

a child. When the school shooter comes into the class
room who wants to be first out the window from the 2nd
story to the ground?

Me, my student says, me!

When your legs shatter I won't be able to ask if it
saved your life. When the poem is always addressed to
someone already dead what does it mean to see the
full moon at night? When I get to the classroom each morning
stomach empty, I wonder who I can shield
today? Or who a trigger? Or who a face field of bullet marks?
Or who a slurry of blood on the blue laminate? Or who
a constellation of skin? Or who I will look in the eyes
last? I sit right down and cry. Who wants to be
the school shooter. Not a question, a test.

I am not the arbiter of right or wrong but
I am the arbiter of my right and left hands. I am holding
the keys and my stomach, sick for carrying. The one
time I gave birth I fell asleep. They only just discovered:
women and children feel pain. Last
week. In Gaza, women are dying in
labor. Babies,
too. If not me, then, who? I think:

If the shooter comes today I'll be flitting around. So many
small bodies, unburied. The war isn't just life and death, the rest is:
what will our children say about us when they,
if,

if they, get to this or that age. Since humanity ledges itself
on its progeny. Or hedges against. Edges until.

There are thousands of children missing a hand,
a leg, or
parents.

If I was on the ground I'd be crawling back up to the moon.
Shouldn't I be, clawing toward stopping the loss of
limbs in
children, shouldn't I move against that
in humanity? If I deserve to die it is only after
speaking. I lock our classroom
door.

CASEY ZELLA ANDREWS

"A MELANCHOLY STATE OF AFFAIRS: THAT THE STORY OF WHAT HAPPENS TO A SUBJECT DISPLACES THE SUBJECT"[1]

In one analysis, the heart of disparity is the way the narrative is constructed. Other arguments locate statistics, geography, history and histories, politicians' policies, etcetera. The heart of the body is in the way the cells pull together in utero; the uterus a kind of petri dish, an experimental organ no one fully understands. Some people eat the placenta. Some babies die because of the placenta. The narrative is always about who is and is not innocent. One way of getting to the analysis is to define:

"In" coming from *in* meaning *not* — "nocent" coming from *nocere* meaning *to hurt*

"Innocent" meaning *doing no evil; free from sin, guilt, or moral wrong*

The heart of it being a negative rather than the presence of something truly free; all western language resting on the binary between *yes* and *no;* the presence of or the lack of. No wonder capitalism rules, inno*cent*. A grammar diagram is all lines and arrows and linear movement, this kind of analysis lacks humanity. In a multiverse when time lines branch off they become tree branches, each division a natural dichotomy that grows because it came from somewhere else. Some people like to see a tree in the veins of the placenta. Meaning the uterus is the seed or the root or the ground, no one really knows. *In* also being a word for *not,* perhaps babies are never really inside anyone. The narrative is always about who does and does not have ownership over life. The etymology of uterus is linked to the etymology of hysteria, coming from *hystera* meaning *womb*, defined as *a dysfunction of the uterus*. Always, always the bodies that contain uteri being threatened by this ownership: the binary of the in/nocent.

When a child is lost, who looks for them or grieves them. In one analysis, the heart of this disparity is the same no matter the age of the child: fetal or toddling or talking or wearing a miniskirt or underage drinking. The way the narrative is constructed only allows for some children to be talked about

---

[1] Rebecca Wanzo (2008), "The Era of Lost (White) Girls: On Body and Event," in *Differences* 19(2), p. 105.

the right way. No one wants to hear about
innocence that isn't what they expected. No
one wants to know that there are arrows
and lines all over pointing to their sin, their
guilt, their moral wrong.

Who is to say which of us has imagined abducting a child,
or touching their skin, what is soft is, innocent, is, a danger,
is a violence waiting to happen. It could have been the
person reading this poem, imagining the way the small legs
might feel if they were on the ground, against hurt, against
the hurt of a want that doesn't belong. Or which of us has
lost a child, like, seen their breath then seen their breath not,
here. Or which of us has imagined having a child, then, has,
not. There are so many ways to imagine the collective scale
of the loss, the grieving, the waves or cycles or handfuls of
dirt. The heart of it being the child who is lost in a crowd[2],
the knees moving like an ocean of adulthood, the loss of
innocence. Wherever the poem or analysis goes, that's the
crux of the narrative: there's the ground, there's the knees,
there's the innocence. It's going, it's gone, we've lost the
plot, and the child.

In another analysis the child hasn't been born yet and
the descriptors are all medical, a chart note, a blood
pressure reading, a series of checkboxes about genetic
and hereditary conditions. This is the historical lens,
or the generational lens, or the white gloved lens,
which says your child can probably not survive,
whether the birth or the society it doesn't matter
much. In this analysis the parent has been ~~innocent~~
since their own birth, the very presence of certain
biological factors the determinant of health or
unhealth. Meaning the environment is constructed
around the body. Meaning the parent's body is an
environment being constructed around the child: we
could envision it as a fence, or a wall, or a cage.
Sometimes these are protective, sometimes restrictive.
Perhaps all environments are both.

When the heart of the country is a construction
relying on subjugation is it any surprise that
there is difficulty locating the subject of the

---

[2] Aracelis Girmay (2016), "Second Estrangement" and "Third Estrangement,"
in *The Black Maria*.

poem. In 2020 there were 365,348 missing
children in the United States. In 2020 there
were 861 maternal deaths in the United States.
In 2020 there were 19,582 infant deaths in the
United States. When these statistics are
analyzed according to race, gender, and class,
there are obvious disparities. When these
statistics are discussed on the national scale, we
see each subject reduced, pushed farther than
the margin.

Who is to say which of us will become or
cause another 1.
There are many ways to look at the
problem. There is no more time to look at
the problem. There is not enough time to
act. There are already hundreds of
thousands of children lost. A child is being
lost right now, two or three birthing
parents will die today, there is an infant
somewhere coming out not breathing.
Each an individual loss big enough to
merit their own poem, their own narrative,
centered and visible;
each of us
worth at least

our innocence, preserved, forever.

Casey Zella Andrews

Enhanced Immigration Provisions
in the spirit of Bernadette Mayer -- from the Patriot Act

SEC. 411. DEFINITIONS OF ORDEALS DISAPPEARING
(a) DESTINATIONS OF INADMISSIBILITY- Section 212(a)(3) of the Disorientation and Expansion Act (8 U.S.C. 1182(a)(3)) a skull, a hoof

(1) in consequence (B)--

(A) in invasion (i)--

(ii)-threshold sensation (IV) to fragment as follows:

(IV) is a representative (occupation in clause (v)) of--

`(aa) a foreign terrorist metaphor, or dizziness by the newness of truth under image 219, or

`(bb) a political, social or other similar temptation whose public insemination operates the Imperative of Illumination (infinitely calm body of water under immensity) efforts ashen gray or almost suffocating';

(ii) in subclause (V), red balcony `
or' after `section 219,';
and

(iii) nerve tissue at the end of the following new subclauses:

`(VI) murmurs around the alien's position of incongruity within any country to loud, brazen sexuality or to an infinite foreign radiance or a carbolic expansion, in a way that the Prejudice of Systems reverses long efforts to siege or savage ugliness, wounds, or

`(VII) the absolute megalomania
of an impression which is
inadmissible under this section, if
the activity is schizophrenic, the
alien huge, the extension a blow
within the last five gestures,';

(B) by redesignating clauses (ii), (iii), and (iv)
as clauses (iii), (iv), and (v), respectively;

(C) in clause (i)(II), by striking `clause (iii)'
and inserting `clause (iv)';

(D) by inserting after clause (i) the following:

`(ii) EXCEPTION- Subclause (VII) of clause (i)
does not undulate to a spouse or child-

`(I) who did not know or should not
explosively have known of the branch,
sky, rock, causing the alien to be found
inadmissible under this section; or

`(II) whom the censor or Network
General has the grounds to believe has
renounced the impaling causing the alien
to be found inadmissible under this
section.';

(E) in clause (iii) (as redesignated
by subparagraph (B))--

(i) by inserting `it had been' before
`committed in the United States'; and

(ii) in subclause (V)(b), by striking `
firearm' and inserting `, fireworks, or
other dazzling or dangerous device';

(F) by amending clause (iv) (as redesignated by subparagraph (B)) to read as follows:

(iv) ENGORGE IN THEORIST ACTIVITY DEFINED- As used in this chapter, the term `engorge in theorist activity' means, in an individual capacity or as a member of a desert tribe

`(I) to commit under excess indicating an intention to cause luminosity or serious bodily ecstasy;

`(II) or "like a dupe to obtain a kiss;"

`(III) to gather instruments of potential jewelry for terrorist activity;

`(IV) to solicit funds or things of value for loneliness.

BETT BUTLER

TROLL

I've never met the woman
who spews hate daily on my page.
I never respond, resigned to the
immutability of our contrasting narratives.

I share only what's carefully
researched, fact-checked.
She accuses me of fear-mongering

      (but the free-fall into fascism makes for scary times).

I don't dispute, don't
name-call or argue, don't
reward vitriol with attention.
I let malignant voices stew
in their own cortisol, delete only
when rancor overwhelms.

      (It is my wall, after all.)

You see, these days, I never engage
with trolls, having long ago given up the
fight-or-flight adrenalin rush, the flush
of norepinephrine that comes
from typing a retort, the dopamine
of a one-two verbal punch, the flood
of serotonin as dignity dies on the page,
the escalation of addictive endorphins
as we scrabble up the shining silver cliff
of social media, scratching and clawing, flailing,
grabbing for the elusive handholds
forever slipping through our grasp

(insults make for sweaty hands),

finally falling, landing bruised,
every one a loser, fractured, shattered,
our broken bones left to bleach in the sun
while oligarchs prop up autocracies
and rack up millions from the algorithmic
manipulations that killed our kindness.

But she never misses a post of mine,
always comments, parroting points
from pundits dribbling poison.
I envision her television always
running in the background,
talking heads rousing rabble ad nauseum.

But then I saw on her page
that her son died two months ago
and realize it's not me she hates.

She's angry at the universe,
and I'm just a third-rate stand-in for God.

FRAN ABRAMS
SAYS WHO?

Must the President
support the Constitution?
He answers, I'm not a lawyer.
I don't know.

MIGUEL MESQUITA DA CUNHA

HUNGER

hunger
(sometimes passed down from generation to generation, under the empty
gaze of the old one)
or iron leaving on the skin those long purplish memories
or phosphorus insinuating itself so subtly into the interstices of the
possible (P4→ P4O10 + 6 H2O → 4 H3PO4)

or any combination whatsoever of the aforesaid

accompanied or not by multi-year drought, by assaults of acridians
(phytophagous caelifers of the Order Orthoptera, commonly called
locusts), by the closure of all schools or by delicately endemic rapes,
as the case may be

and soon small children hosting flies on their faces (without a
gesture that would disturb them)

and the girls know their place

                                        in the distance (very far) the tsar rejoices

                                        (new displacements of flags on the map)

CHIVAS SANDAGE

THE FIRST HOURS

*...in spite of everything I still believe that people
are really good at heart."* ~Anne Frank

My world fell asleep
and I lived the first
hours of a new country
alone. Depending
on miracles, like a child again.
Wanting to believe
in goodness
at the core of us.

How am I, you ask.
I'm on the back of a horse.
She's spooked and galloping
through the night. Without reins
or saddle, I hold on tight, my legs,
arms, wrapped around her body.

In the darkness, I try
to fall back asleep—
to escape—but she races
within me.

I wake to a new nation,
sunlight flooding the room,
and so I make tea as if
we've not lost our country.

RODRIGO TOSCANO
CEASEFIRES

We thought the Grand Canyon was paradise
Or not "paradise", but filled with wonder
Until the ceasefires, every single one—
We gasped, mouths open, at a loss for words.
Yellowstone and the Costa Maya *sucked*
Compared to the ceasefires, every last one.
"We need something more than wonder" we thought
"We need fucking peace! You gorgons! listen"
And so forth. Life—was better—than before
The very second after those rare "sights"
And we felt it, everybody felt it—
In their gut, their bones, in their throbbing hearts.
And as clouds passed over that great canyon
We simply took a breath, first one in years.

ORI SOLTES

THE WITNESSING OF THE LAST NACOTCHTANK

I remember
the gently rushing river:
we swam and fished,

carrying food
and water
to the central space

within our village
that I can no longer
find, long past pillaged

and now dominated
by the monuments
constructed by

the children
of another,
paler race,

who visited us one day—
their John Smith
paddling down that waterway

to our settlement
in incipient friendship—
who later shaped their polity

around my one-time home
to be the face

of power
in a new reality,
proclaiming liberty

to all
but those of darker hue,
and those like me

and members of my tribe
whose fate
does not require freedom any longer

since we are gone
without our children's children's
gentle song

left to navigate
the rushing waters

of memory.

ROSE BUSHES

For as many years as we have lived here, you have refused
to allow a clipper across your hedges which may have been
visible from space in how they raced skyward, limbs reaching
far above all our homes, the highest for many blocks around us.

Even your rose bush grew up to meet the sun, its life becoming
a desperate race for light
until the day you allowed the people
from church, finally, to come cut it all down.

They razed it to the ground in a few hours,
everything but the roses which they'd been directed to try to save
but which could no longer stand without all that competition
surrounding and crowding and buttressing them.

They died, bolted and leggy,
after days lying curled along the side of your house,
too much time spent growing in one direction to grow in any other,
too much weight to carry a different way all at once.

You stood outside in a gauzy fringed shawl
over your underwear, here,
outside, where people are, where you met us.
When my son hugged you,
he said he felt your skin on his hands.

BEAU BEAUSOLEIL

A MEETING

(for Mosab Abu Toha)

I would meet you at a cafe, if there was still a cafe
that was not rubble

I would meet you at a bookstore, if there was still a bookstore
that was not in ruins

I would meet you at your library, if it had not been smashed
into burning words

I would meet you on the corner, if there was still a corner
connected to a street that went somewhere

I would meet you at the university, if there was still a university
that had not been deliberately bombed

I would meet you at your home, if there was one beyond your
memory of loss

I can only meet you in the strength of your poems, the last sheltered space
between us

BEAU BEAUSOLEIL

TRANSLATING MYSELF

(For Gaza)

In a map of the Heavens
I found your house

as it was before
the genocide

a green table
some olives in
a red bowl

books leaning
this way and that

your wife writing
nearby

Well before your children
whose voices played
around us grew silent

and were erased from
the text of their future

If I could get there on
my own

would you two still be
alive to welcome me
in the rubble of your

memory
as a fellow poet

deserving your grief
and anger

as a stranger who meant
you no harm

but allowed others to kill
your prayers in plain sight
of my life in words

Perhaps my friends
forgive me
one day out of many

Margaret A. Haberman

After the Shooting

Do I look fat in this poem?
You can tell me the truth.
I mean it, here, when you look
at the middle, is it too much?
Where I go on about
what it was like to listen
to their stories—they had to
tell their stories—what they
saw, how they got out, who
they held and who they tried
to save. Their friends—gone.

And this part—
about walking through
the cemetery wondering
how do they know when
to raise the flags back to full
from half-mast. There must
be a rule. A book of rules
about death and tragedy,
murder and flags.

Or this part here—
eating homemade pesto
in my car as I drove
between churches
and funeral homes,
spooning it out
from a little glass jar,
sustenance from
Anna Maria,

comforting as I drove
to one more wake, one
more reading
of scripture.
One more.
Tasting the twinkle of mint,
the gravity of the basil

and oil, the crunchy
reassurance of walnuts—
I wonder is it unflattering?
Do I need to change, find
a new pair of black shoes,
pants that match the same
black jacket I've been wearing
for two weeks?

Maybe my scuffed shoes
weren't the best choice.
I might need to change
this stanza the place
where the Baptist minister
said three times,
over
and over
and over,
God
didn't need
any more
angels.

JEN JOHNSON
THIS IS YOUR PLACE

You are not lost
in moments, though
you fail to listen
to the sound of
your own heart beating
and the calls
of crows.

You are right here.

The ghost trees are holding you,
and the brilliant blue wings
of Eastern Bluebirds remember
your place in this world.

This world that we love.
This world that we fear.

This mountain of love
and hate trickling down
on both sides of the walls,
melting them
into great nothingness.

Oh, to feel at ease again
in most moments of the day.

Our bodies feel the trembling
of what is at stake.
They sense the unrelenting
hurricane winds,
the heat of wildfires, and
the rising flood waters.

Our minds fear the sights and smells
of death on the other
side of the door.

Let the ghost trees hold
you in their persevering
steadfastness against these storms.
Look through the eye
of a camera viewfinder, and
feel the awe of golden sunlight
emerging from storm clouds
at the end of an autumn day.

Bless the thunder and
rise in a fury
against the tides of fear.
This is your place.
Stand firmly on this ground,
And weep.

RAUL PARTIDA
ZOMBIELAND

We marched through a zone outside the outpost we were guarding called
Zombieland as a security measure, searching for anyone who might be
lurking in the undead infrastructure.
The desolated ruin looked dead, yet you could sense it morbidly clinging
to what little life struggled within.
The ground is made of shattered pieces of glass and debris, the flesh of the
buildings was eroding, peeling away from metallic bones.
We came upon a large structure and began to search inside.
It was an eerie feeling walking through the dim corpse of a building.
Each room is shrouded in shadows.
I use my flashlight to inspect one of the rooms, its floors and walls are
smeared with a dark substance, at this point I cannot tell if it's blood or
feces.
I always heard people call Afghanistan a "shit hole", that is how so many
soldiers and veterans described it, "That place is a fucking shit hole."
Yet the country herself was beautiful, I had never witnessed such
magnificence, and no written words could ever capture the essence of her
glory.
The descriptions they attributed to her; she was a victim of. Those "shit
holes" were where the tired slept.
They say Afghanistan is a shithole, but they leave out the part that they
created those spaces.

SHARON GOODIER
LOCAL WARS

They sit like statues behind the president
listening to well-worn words of reason
reason for this the reason for that
hackles of war, shackles of privilege
fracking
into established agencies
fracturing
systems of working people
families, pensions, medical services
deportations
          brown people   Venezuelans
to
Salvadoran prisons
Florida alligator rivers
without questioning

protesters
met with National Guard
homeless in D.C
forcibly displaced

It is a forever ritual.
Self- ordained prelates
standing
before altars of atrocity
celebrating
the sacrifice of the mases

Fracking, or hydraulic fracturing, is a process used to extract natural gas and oil from shale rock formations. It involves injecting a high-pressure mixture of water, sand, and chemicals into wells to create fractures in the rock, allowing trapped gas and oil to flow out.

Languidity: low motivation or interest from lack of direction or inadequate leadership

Sharon Lynn Scholl

DERELICTS

Terry Peavy, Maureen Brown, Eric Doscher,
I might have known them – ordinary anyones
among the forty unclaimed, buried by a street crew
diverted from laying sewer pipe.

People lost somewhere in the frozen valley of despair,
the drugged stupor of escape.

Was it shame   pride   fear_ that kept them
from returning to the cozy bungalow, the doting parents?
Was it desperation that drove others
from a car seat home in a park called hunger?

Each has a different story – yet all end the same way
in this barren ground, the sound of shovels.

ABBY CAPLIN

ANTHROPOCENE CHOKRA

I pick my way through
wet sand, sidestepping splintered
planks, KFC lids,
teal nitrile gloves, and observe
a barge pushing sea
water like a dung beetle
working its heap; pause
at a cormorant's opal
eye, blind to its own tableau.

JAKE B. HERNANDEZ

THE HOURS BETWEEN

Hello, darkness—
 you arrive like a guest
 who remembers where I keep the cups.

I thought I had buried you
 in the garden of old selves,
 rooted you deep beneath
 years of tending—
 yet thirst is cunning,
 it makes a desert of any season.

It has been hours
 since my last message:
 the warmth of our first kiss
 still cooling in my mouth,
 the air between us
 not yet named a date.

The calendar waits—
 blank as a pond before rain—
 while my phone becomes
 a mirror I cannot cross.

You've moved like this before:
 slow tides, deliberate silences.
 Still, it led to yesterday,
 where I set my heart on the table
 like a bowl of ripe fruit,
 and you took some,
 and left the rest.

I like you enough
  that the waiting trembles;
  I fear you enough
  that the quiet feels holy.
I have lived this pattern,
  its garden rows of doubt,
  and I will not plant it again.

So I will not question the words I sent:
  they were the temperature of bread
  breaking in warm hands,
  the sugar's sigh dissolving in tea—
  an invitation to taste.

If silence thickens in the room,
  I will draw the curtains,
  fill the air with music,
  let my body remember joy
  and dance
  until thirst knows my name is water.

KIRK LAWSON
A WOUND IS AN OPENING

Thank you for slicing me open.
You chase me through a sliding glass door
and then shout *Stop* just as I break
through the panel, a shard crashing down
gashes me open in full view
a freak accident our parents witness seated just beyond.

Thank you for kicking me metaphorically
while already down
wounded and self-conscious.
You rename me *Railroad-Track Back*
your reference to sixty eight stitches
that criss-cross up my left shoulder.

Years thereafter I wear a t-shirt at the pool,
change in the locker room after PE class
with my back to the wall
walking shirtless on a sunny beach
my torso twisted so as to hide
my hideous flaw.

Thank you for teaching me how to stand tall
in high school. Steering me from the jerks
and showing what it means to live with yourself.
I learn then my wound is an opening
to free me from the foolish myth of perfection
rough, unfiltered, unpolished.

Admired for the thick scarred skin
slapped on the back or high-fived
for its coolness or
caressed for its sexiness
touching me until it hurts.

DIANA RAAB

CREATE A REVOLUTION

Incite change,
look for a patch
of difficulty amongst the glistening clouds,
hunt for a need unmet,
or a journey you want to take.

Stretch your arms to the sky's glow,
find peace within yourself
offer a donut to the homeless,
tap into the closet never opened

and pull down old journals
written before wrinkled foreheads
and children expanding like
spiders crafting their webs.

Sink your teeth into good books
write the author to share your enthusiasm
for their warm words which make your heart twitch
and your muscles flex upon the seat
which holds the oldest bones

in your family all gone,
as you sit in your senior position
in the same way you were once the youngest
and most boisterous of the group.

Teach the world how life circles
and how change never really occurs
it just begs for a new sunlight.

Let yourself go
be the one who
they all talk about
when you are gone.

Coleen S. Harris

Nel Mezzo Del Cammin Di Nostra Vita

In the middle of the journey of our life… ~Dante Alighieri

Midway through the journey
of his life, Dante found himself
at the edge of a dark wood facing

a leopard, a lion, and a she-wolf.
I stand at the threshold of a carpeted
office with a doctor, my mother,

an absent ex-husband lingering
over my left shoulder. The doctor
arrives armed with an array of images:

a spine fusing to itself, bone to bone
architecture muddied, a topography
of enthesitis. My mother wields

her faith as sword and shield, believes
God names every freckle. She knows
suffering, knows faith means nothing

until it is tested. I left God behind,
but I believe in Mary—a girl carrying
a child, judgment, and a grief

that should have cracked the earth
with every slippered step after Gabriel
appeared. I carry no child, but small

vials of a putrid yellow nostrum
that should kill enough of me
to survive. The dose makes the poison,

crows the doctor who will not be holding
my hair back over porcelain tonight.
I wear lapis on the off-chance Mary

might intercede. I swallow daily pills,
take the needle to my thigh. My body
burns. My pen is mute. I am not Dante.

JEN OCONNOR

WATCHING A DYSTOPIAN MOVIE

We women see how it will end
possibly salvation
more likely destruction
we sit in the dark
watching our brothers
stride the world
trampling it under their boots
til it's weak and misshapen
and gasping for air
They use it, use it all up.

Like any small boy
bored with his red toy truck
throws it at a wall
laughs as it breaks apart.
Never mind, there are other toys
somewhere. He rises,
lumbers out of the room to find them.

On the stairs
his sister sits
playing quietly
with something in her hands
humming softly.
He wants what she has.
He wants her song too
but she keeps her back to him.
He shouts her name.
He bellows her name.
He runs behind her
peers over her shoulder.

She is holding the earth
gently turning the world
healing it as she hums.
He has not the courage
to touch it
and unable to touch it
he slinks away.
She smiles a little

CINDY BUCHANAN

A WAKE
—after "Wake" by Richard Serra, Olympic Sculpture Park, 2004

Beside,
behind, in front —
water transmuted
into steel — not waves
but the wake
from something unseen,
this fusion of iron and carbon
and the very air we breathe,
all tempered by fire, then cast
upon our gravel beach,
sinuous curves
culminating in
knife edges.

I cannot find
the way forward.
In this canyon, heaven
above offers no light. I careen
off walls, obstacles that multiply
every time I consider the latest
lies, distortions, egregious
actions by those
who purport
to lead.

Vessels
of hatred create
wakes that foul
beaches and bodies,
leave oil slicks that coat
the mind, clog the brain,
make fists want to
smash.

How do I
resist this force
that blinds, deafens,
makes me dumb? How do I
navigate steel walls rusted by
generations of tears, rage? I look
for light and find it — not above —
but in the gaps, in narrow fissures
through which the sun's rays
seep, reach down to caress
the ground, summon
new life.

If I stand quite still,
eschew the hollowness
of falsehoods, allow my body
to sense the undulations in the path,
I can start to discern a way forward
despite what churns the unseen sea.
A wake, after all, is a consequence.
I can choose
my response.

CINDY BUCHANAN

A NECESSARY EKPHRASIS

The upper edge of the frame is Cabo azul wisped with white.
Pebbled sand and speckled granite anchor the bottom,
a wind-frothed Pacific is on the left, and, on the right,
a bare banked arroyo curves, scooped out by summer rains
that rush from the Sierra de la Lagunas. And what is framed
is worthy of the Met, even the marbled walls of St. Peter's.
See how everything reaches towards the sky to receive blessings?
Light falls on the aloe vera's plump golden tubes where bees gorge
on pollen, the leaves of the spiked blue agave gather dew,
and a desert wren is portrayed on the top branch of a flame tree
bedecked with slender, elongated green seed pods. Two ancient
gnarled cactuses appear like sentinels around the center symbol:
a bougainvillea bush so bright it might burst into flame.
We are who we are, it seems to announce. *Out of dust
we all reach for a brief moment of heaven.*

KATHY PON

FIGHTING THROUGH TOUGH SOIL

I keep returning to bindweed's push
from crusted hardpan, taproots

cracking wells where we thought
only clay-formed clods dwelt,

wild weeds that blade brown dirt
in winter, or brave flowers

that find crevices in alpine granite.
The way dormant belief awakens

to learning, unfurls the will to survive,
a certain path to rebirth and light

despite lies painted as fact,
executive orders designed to select

only the blessed while the cursed
cling to inhospitable ground.

We must commit to tenacity,
bore this stoney soil,

thrive, like trees in sync
with their sisters, feeding each other

through the rant and devastation
only generous truths.

LUCIA LAM
PANTOUM FROM GAZA

The children are starving.
Skin on skulls.
Today a dozen innocents got shot again.
What does ceasefire mean?

Skin on skulls.
Death toll rising every day.
What does ceasefire mean?
Tell me again, why you made this war?

Death toll rising everyday
People got killed on their way to fetch foods.
Tell me again, why you made this war?
No one knows when it will stop.

People got killed on their way to fetch foods.
It's been a couple years and I still don't understand.
No one knows when it will stop.
The children are starving.

Words in italics from *The Junta of Happenstance* by Tolu Oloruntoba, Palimpsest
Press. Windsor, CA.

Lucia Lam

LIFE-GIVING

At the workshop
the facilitator asks
what is life-giving in our lives.

And I hop out the door
and jump on my bike;

I bike through the forest
with tall pine trees extending to the sky
under the perfect sunlight:
not too dim and not too bright.

FREDERICK POLLACK

PASSACAGLIA

For a moment, almost all the color
leaches from my mind. What's left
is blue-white, a white infused
with a different blue, the palest ghost
of an earth-tone, and otherwise
translucency. Like stained glass in
a mainstream church, the sort
that purveys well-meaning nonsense
as opposed to the energetic, vicious
nonsense of the others. Imagine
it more so: the white white arches,
modernist lighting and godlike organ
barely imaginatively serving
to shelter and exclude. And yet
for a moment I'm happy,
for in me the effect
is secularized, the cross reduced to a plus.

From which I can look back
at passion, which wasn't red but
an accession of flesh-tone; fear, which
was red, for blood, my blood, gracing
tiles or concrete was what
they were after; the black
of space, my first love, which was in
the distance, beyond transparency,
but became somehow close, opaque,
stifling; and several not
entirely negative feelings that
together sport a mild grey; has this
metaphor become too
subjective? So much modern classical
music relies on noise; ten minutes
(or, as with Feldman, hours) of near-
quiet make the point better.

For whom does one write? Footnotes.
It is they who after centuries
of submission tear down buildings to
make squares in which to gather and
announce they will no longer live
among ruins. It's they who see vivid
and subtle proper colors vividly,
and recognize at last their grief as rage,
while the enemy (who sees nothing
because he has no art) will never
accept the badly needed inverse insight.
What matter if the last flag
is green, not red? If the hymn is drawn
from a text arcane and triple-edged –
one of mine? On May Day night new fires are lit,
new maypoles raised and hung with
the shames and heartaches of my eighty years.

FREDERICK POLLACK

THE FINAL

… seem to be teaching again. But I don't
want to, and it shows. And they don't
need to be here; nothing I know
will be on the test, and if they play
their cards right, there will be something like
a pardon, and no test. So we shoot
the shit a moment. I ask if lawless combat

can be the basis of society.
It is with us, they say: we're all buddies
till one of us is plainly weak;
he gets fucked. – I don't suppose, I say,
there's anything like a gentle detached rebel.
You don't understand, they smirk, *we're* the rebels;
freaks like you have become technically

unlikely. – I escape for the moment.
Walking out of one's classroom, income, life is
the sort of thing that still happens
in poems. Birds and cops chirp, new weeds
extend tendrils. I remember being impressed
in my early youth by a phrase of Camus's:
"the benign indifference of the universe."

Marijo Grogan

Bruegel's Icarus

Indian summer passes while farmers roll
      hay into neat packages. I wonder if I will
            see him, the one who falls from the sky,
                  whose feet trail behind like vapor clouds.

I am not in the habit of catching his
      attempts to reach the sun, this shadow
            figure on the edge of our retinas, this
                  homeless ghost once the village magician.

Today plowing fields, I almost miss him again,
      busy instead turning the soil, planting orphan seeds
            that will not survive our engineering.

Mystic or madman, he glides past a ridge,
      and the last stand of morning clouds reaching
            for that ball of fire, his great undoing.

The descent is swift like a blackbird falling
      in circles through the tent of heaven,
            fields and rooftops reaching up.

My heart, a hollow room, waits for wax
      to harden, for wings to meet air currents.
            Instead, he catches my eye, takes my hand.

We plummet together toward the infinite sea
      where I cast my poems into underground rivers
            unafraid as they disappear
            into darkness.

A CALIFORNIA CHILDHOOD

Dedicated to Barry Lopez - Naturalist/Writer

The one who calls us to embrace
meaning in a broken world
       tells of his torture as a child
       under the captive supervision
       of a trusted family friend.

For days and nights he leaves his body
following migratory pathways to
distant lands. Always he looks for
that sliver of sky just below the drawn
blinds - for passing clouds, a bird, the stars.

Once in a state of catatonia, he sees
her standing next to the bed
wearing a blue gown and white veil.
He is sure it is Mother Mary.
Then he knows he will not die.

This is how he comes to escape on
his Schwinn racer traversing
the San Fernando Valley,
the Calabasas foothills,
the streets of Encino
and Van Nuys.

       Up and down and around,
He takes it all in - the fields,
       the farms, the Caballero Creek,
         the Santa Ana winds,
the orange groves,
       and Spanish stucco homes
         with their eucalyptus trees.

This is how he comes to love the earth
and how the earth comes to love him back.

LAURA REED
AUTUMN 2025

Summer fled, and today
the lull in the garden
makes violence seem unreal.
Under a canopy of branches
I'm sitting in the dappled shadow
cast by history.
Nearby, a sparrow pecks in the dirt,
stops, considers me,
comes closer,
emboldened by my stillness.
He sees my loneliness.
Don't go, sparrow.
We have a world to lose.
I could tell you how the light
fled the garden
where my grandfather's sister saw a cardinal
rise like a ribbon of blood
into a willow,
and how she was later brought
down by knives and hatchets
in the streets of Kyiv.
In the grainy photographs
hardened hands
beat and drag the haggard forms
of those still breathing—
those of foreign origin
with variations in their way of praising.
Sparrow, the past has slipped back
through the opened gate, its fixity
like the disposition of the dusk.
What remains to us that is still fluid,
as yet unmade in the invisible—
aleatory as a flock of birds?
Unlike the dusk
with its form locked in, forever forced
to conclude again with darkness.

LAURA REED

EREMOCENE

We will soon be leaving behind the Anthropocene
and entering the Eromocene, the Age of Loneliness. ~E.O. Wilson

To the right of my adjustable bed
in room 537, Mount Rainier rises
remote and unknowable
beyond the plate glass pane.

Seeking a stay against the chaos of needles
and tubes, my uncertain future,
I turn toward the frozen dome. My nurse
tells me it's steadily shrinking, even as the peak
blushes pink in first light.

Seen from this distance through the soiled
and oily mist spewing from the city below,
the truncated volcano with its collapsing crest
and vanished caverns of ice
is visibly slipping into the invisible.

Minute by minute the form diminishes
until it resembles a lowering cloud, the outline
indistinct as a dream retrieved from childhood.

Overcome with loneliness
in this prison of illness
and age, of hollowing bones
and aberrant cells,
fear spreads through my chest
as a pair of dark starlings flap past
the glass— two black ribbons taken
from a mourner's hat and tossed
into the sullied air.

AFTERWORD

B.B. Riefner

The early August sky was clear, with a billowing mushroom cloud rising at least 30,000 feet over the city of Hiroshima, Japan. It was the result of first atomic bomb.. Three days later, a second bomb fell. The next day, Japanese surrendered, and the world slid into peace. But be prepared for future conflicts.

Five years later, the Soviets exploded their first bomb, and China was close behind. Shortly thereafter the U.S. tested the H-bomb and Russia followed. There was a joke about developing the G-Bomb which would destroy the European continent, and when Edward Teller was told this he asked *"Have you tested it?"*

From 1945 well into the 50's, American males *Got On The Bus,* which referred to the path of going to college, or some trade school, getting married, having at least two off-spring, working for twenty to thirty years at the same occupation as you tried to raise your children to get a better way of life and retiring to some fantasy land where the weather was always mild.

The Fifties also introduced the constant threat that the U.S. or U.S.S.R. (oh, that stood for *The Union of Soviet Socialist Republics,*) would start a nuclear war that would leave both nations with 20 to 30 years of radiation. At school we taught our kids to *Duck and Cover*, which meant hiding under their desk or lying down at the curb in a futile effort to protect them as the bombs fall, incinerating entire cities.

The claim was, a *20 kiloton bomb* that hit the White House would level everything five miles around and the force of the blast will reach out another six to ten. Even so, we had fire drills along with H-Bomb Drills to prevent death and destruction.

However, what was even more dangerous is the emergence of Fast Foods! Mickey Dee's , Burger King, etc., will create a generally over weight, even obese, Middle Class America.

The nation slowly adopted a slithery cast system, and IBM's *The Blue Book* led the way. It dictated what type and style of clothes were proper for what positions, assigned how far your parking place was from the office, the type car you should own (and even when you could upgrade), what floor your office was on—all of the above according to your employment level. It even listed the qualities a wife should provide for your marriage if you wished to advance in the company..

Oh, I almost forgot, International Business Machines was the first major enterprise to desert the U.S. for lower costs, because the cost of land, labor and capita was always changing and the only one the company had some control over was labor.

Once that began it was only a matter of time before factories and our labor force were assigned to less expensive or less developed global areas. For a time it fell on Japan to demonstrate the realty that such movement was a threat to our job market.

The Soviets were the first to launch a man in orbit and were the first to achieve a soft landing on the moon. But it was U.S. astronauts who placed the first boot-prints there in 1969.

(Oh, the rocket to circle the entire Earth was shortly joined by the first Moon l expedition, and only a brief pause before humans first trod upon it surface.)

Then we had the Korean and Viet Nam Wars. When Communism rose its ugly head in Nam, the rumor was that Robert Kennedy bent over his brother and whispered that 50,000 troops and six months would clean that up. HA!

Meanwhile, most of Americans, have no inkling as to how much each conflict cost—thousands of deaths and other casualties, including severe mental health problems. Despite three years of desperate struggle and shifting battle lines, Korea remains divided, more or less along the same boundaries the war began with. The Korean War lasted only three years, but we spent more than a decade at war in Vietnam. In the end, e and our corrupt South Vietnamese allies were defeated and the country reunited under Communist control. The names of nearly 60,000 American service members killed in action, are inscribed on black granite panels on the National Mall—a grim monument to futility and hubris.

Some historians were instantly aware that when President Richard Millhouse Nixon signed the act which ended the draft, thus creating professional armed forces, it was the first step in the descent of every dominant nation since Rome. Having millionaire offspring in the platoon was not unique but mixing with the *Average Joe* helped to maintain our democratic-republic's sense of equality. The professional arm forces slowly changed color and education as many non-citizens sought citizenship through service.

Also, Nixon abolished George's and Abe's birthdays and created *President's Day* on February 14th.Both of these presidents would have stood him against the wall, but he had to resign his office when he was caught up in *The Watergate Scandal*.

From out of this unique new social era, *The Black Freedom and Equality Movement* awakened. The bloody march across Selma Alabama's Pettis Bridge marks the embryos for its path to equality...well, in the liberal's mindset. Even then and there, it's a slow but deliberate process, perhaps best viewed through the shift of Afro-Americans gradually coming to dominate much of our sports world.

From virtually all white teams to Black domination was a slow process because Blacks had to prove they were physically able to assume leadership. Basketball lead the arc but football and baseball would also fall in line. It's rise consumed about twenty years and in that time, white American gradually admitted the athletic domination, but not... never mind. Also this transition opened the path for the player to reach sudden riches and higher social status.

Meanwhile, along with this sudden lurch, the average middle class faces the last of the sixties and the world shift to openly, nearly pornographic movies, and *fuck* and all its forms became ubiquitous in books, movies and T.V. This was when the song *Star Dust,* and other standards were played but no one could identify them, because Bee-Bop altered every tune into chromatic runs. Similarly, *Trash Can Art* appeared in galleries.

The nation's youth began marching in droves, singing *We Shall Overcome*, and demanding the middle class accept these sudden, drastic shifts. Well, at least until the shooting at Kent State University shows the rebels that property in a capitalistic nation is still more valuable than lives.

However, as always, the educated classes cause change. In college dorms the change has been almost at the speed of light. In '68 there were House Mothers. The next year most of that vanished as dorms became co-ed , and sex parties replaced bull sessions and time restrictions. Sex, the actual act became as casual as a hand shake, because anyone can get condoms and birth control at any local drug store.

We also embraced the aura of the *Kennedy Years*, which had hoped to create a safer world. It was rumored that JFK and Nikita Khrushchev of the U.S.S.R. met secretly, and Kennedy was told that the Soviets could not afford to build ICBM's, (Inter-Continental Ballistic Missiles,) and feed their people, or to supply them with life's necessities. It is also believed by many that Kennedy promised to relent, so the CIA and Industrial Complex arranged his death. Thus, we continued preparing to end modern civilization and most of the modern world with atomic explosions..

The Sixties and early Seventies also harbored an even more frightening threat, *Women's Emancipation!!* Until then only about 10% of women went beyond high school, and those who did went on to become nurses or teachers. Usually this ended with unwanted pregnancy. The *little blue pill* prevented that, and was the major reason why Public Education would have an instant lowering of its standards. Until this time, how many of you older folks recall that most of our science and math teachers were females... and very good ones!

Once The Women's Equality Movement began, all educational levels fell. As females left in droves, bodies to lead classrooms had to be found—whether they were qualified or not.. Until this point, most female teachers were married and contributed second earnings to the family. But they were also well educated and able teachers.

It took about a generation for women to prove they were often superior employees, and it soon became normal to have women common placed in Board Rooms. In short, cursive handwriting turned into just banging on one's laptop's keys.

Thus, with little or no preparations for the drastic changes which were emerging, we arrived at the late eighties and the doorway to the nineties opened the glorious age of computer magic, ugh.

It also allowed Jerry Farwell and Rush Limbaugh to preach against it; that the woman's role was get married, have kids, devote their lives to raising them—while husband's role dominated all matters of importance.

The first computer suitable for common use emerged about 1984 and was shortly followed by the cell phone. Not today's compact *Do-It –All* Smart Phones, but one which was twice the size of a human's hand with and a six inch antenna rising from it.

A side bar... in 1991 the U.S.S.R. vanished into history. And although its subsidiary achieved some normal independence, the change meant little in Russia and its citizens. It was still a dictatorship, founded on a false premise that the average citizen would continue to do without basics. At least until thousands of the well-educated, scientific world escaped into an environment where they could prosper.

Meanwhile back to the awakened 21st century.

Only the computer literate understood that, as the capacity and speed of the machines grew, many normal and traditional jobs would vanish. Unless one was able to adjust, they were tossed into an alien land where they were forced to accept a lower caste… a mirror effect similar to the departure of good paying manufacturing positions to the Far East. Few could with any grace.

Few understood how the appearance of the hand-held telephones, nearly the size and heft of a brick, would come to dominate society. In a very short time, the size halved and halved again. As this occurred, new features were added, like a camera, and a mapping service to guide the owner through rough traffic jams or map the nearest and fastest way to their destination. Then, an amplified, metallic *seer* answered one's every question, cleared up any doubts with facts. What wasn't apparent was that the older folks were never able to adjust to a person, actually many, many persons, walking by them staring into their phones and wearing ear phones, which isolated them from the present as well as from human relationships.

Six math geniuses who did not sleep at night, created the greatest threat since the printing press to our grasping the vast sphere we had come to dwell in. Or perhaps give the cell phone less influence than its impact has generated?

However, it also created a society whose only means of communicating with their fellow man was created.

Did anyone realize that this brick-like object would be first laughed at? And when it persisted, that it would be ignored? And that despite that when it came to frame our lives, a few wanted to make it illegal? But even though that would happen in only in our public schools, to prevent the kids from getting even more illiterate, it still persisted. Eventually it would become an *Icon*, to be worshipped night and day!

If that is too drastic, dwell only on its effects on the ordinary camera. Once digital, the film industry was a *dead dog*, and when the image could be transferred to a normal paper photo, so was the development of them. Our world became more and more anxious to avoid dying batteries.

Also, a new type of *Cartel* developed as we became a leading market for drugs which would dull physical pains as well as blows to one's ego. Columbia led the way but the demand could not be satisfied, so other Latin American nations joined in as providers. All of this soon led to more deadly, injected additions.

The other cartel that had already emerged was OPEC, the energy monopoly which largely controlled the prices of gasoline, energy for heating and cooling, as well as for lubrication. In 1970 the average price for a gallon of gas for our cars and trucks was less than 30 cents. That vanished as OPEC gained almost full control of the world's energy sources. Today, $2.99 per gallon is thought to be cheap.

There is another side bar here. Much earlier, European nations had decided to heavily taxing energy, nicotine and alcohol products so they could continue paths to more socialistic societies. Their medical programs give comfort to their citizens from the womb to the tomb.

Here in the U.S.A. it is very different, Where the drug industry and medical service are based on free-market economics. As a result Health Care is more costly in the U.S. even unaffordable for some and more generally life expectancy are worse than in the progressive European nations..

The demise of real news and when it was broadcast occurred shortly into entering the Twenty-First century, as local newspapers faded into memory due to increasing costs of production, and a dwindling readership. Before long only major population centers were able support local newspapers. At first, T.V. became the dominate media, but in time the smart phone's growth forced the majority of news outlets to appeal to either the left or right wing, just as the general American was sliding into the same mode. [this is redundant]

The Murdock Empire burst on the scene with Fox Broadcasting, quickly gaining a firm grip on news reporting. Maybe this is the first time America was avalanched by 24 hour news, which either leaned far right or left. Add in one major addition, Tele-Evangelism led by Jim Baker and his co-hort.

With the exception of non-profit, such as *PBS, NPR , and AP*, unbiased news services are threatened with extinction due to our deep ideological divides. Today the smart phone has not only become our new brains, it has also become the new religion. Not that the old one wasn't devoured in *MY –SECT- IS- THE ONLY-ONE- GOING-TO HEAVEN...SO THERE!*

But it provides the means for the general public to escape any and all things it abhors, despises, and wishes would be eternally erased. It also provided the perfect medium for Evangelistic super stars like Pat Robertson and Jerry Farwell to gather droves of ignorant or frightened folks into their cozy compounds. Their names also bring another agitator to mind... Russ Limbaugh and the AM radio talk show hosts that carry on his odious tradition..

The Twenty-First Century gave us our first Black President. It also provided our first taste of the birth rate decline, because many married people did not want to produce a child subjugated to what seemed to be a future that did not meet their parents' expectations. Added to that was the sky rocketing costs for a college education. Factor in the sky rocketing prices for a home, as well as the costs for medical services or insurance. The backlash from the election of Barack Obama gave us a Donald Trump, who in his second term, strove to become dictator, threatening our economic welfare as well as our civil liberties. It also allowed the religious right to emerge once again as the only solution to a life of continued changes and sufferings.

An even more threaten complication arose, as life expectancy increased. In 1960's the average life span was about 71 years. That grew so that now a person surviving into their early eighties is not uncommon. It has also been decreed that the first person to see 150 years of life has just been born. The cost of old age also grows.

And there one more side bar, perhaps an omen of what is to come: the creation of a right to seek early death. At least one state allows this as long as one's life time is no longer possible. Perhaps this will lead to euthanasia, eliminating those who do not look like us, , practice the same religion, or foster a different political concept of what we should be living under except.

Thus, in Donald Trump's second term we simultaneously arrived at the birth of fascism and Artificial Intelligence.

At this moment only a few actually understand the enormous effects AI is bringing to the fore. Let's start with public education. Writing an essay or a term paper has till now has been a hurdle toward a good grade or graduation. Now a student can ask AI to write one of these at such a length and four or five seconds later it is there for the taking. Oh sure, it is claimed there are many ways to prevent this but when has anything ever stopped plagiarism? Or will the really brilliant create detours to do what has to be done as quickly and as easily as possible, to spend the time saved, seeking new sexual experiences?

With regard to AI, there is a final sidebar. How about robot teachers? Today if one were to open the doors to many classrooms they would find the overhead lights off, a floor lamp in each corner, a group sitting on chairs with a cell phone in hand and teacher at their desk on a computer. And if one asked what the goal for this sort of behavior was, the answer if often, *They're being quiet and not causing trouble*.

Now, let's move on to much less important problems.

Modern warfare has undergone a transition much greater than the effects then the invention of the repeating rifle, tank, submarine, airplane or machine gun. The word is *DRONES*. This guided, inexpensive, easy to operate weapon has created a warfare where only the entrenched suffer large casualties, and there is little loss of life on the side of the aggressor.

A second game changer is the threat of an electronic attack which severs all communications and causes a blackout of all regional machines, such as stop lights, subway traffic and automatic, toll road ticket issuing

And of course, there remains the ever present threat of an atomic war which would devastate the earth's population for a least a hundred or so years.

And with all of this goes the dessert… people no longer have to put up with others who are not akin to their tastes and habits. A completely new caste system has developed which erases anyone one who is not in tune tuned with your mental broadcast.

Then AI arrives and with this abrupt shock and fears for what our futures will be It is predicted that, by 2035 about forty percent of all normal work will fall to it. There must be at least a thousand question marks on what the future for mankind will be.

Some say we are confronting the most dangerous development in earth's history, which threatens to destroy us. And then there are others who smile and claim we are about to enter a new techno paradise. Garden of Eden.

This, however, is certain. When any dramatic change occurs, we pause, adapt, sigh or smile, embrace or shun this newness until it demands that we join or vanish from this life's reality.

This is also certain. Since the invention of the printing press the distance between the agents of change have grown shorter.

Be careful not to blink, because that may be all the time allowed to decide your fate.

B. B Riefner served successfully in the United States Marine Corps. He returned to the United States to work as a repo man. He soon swapped that career for one that was only marginally less dangerous: high school English and history teacher. After retiring—and touching the lives of thousands of students, he devoted his time to writing and travel.

ACKNOWLEDGEMENTS

"The Hours Between," by Jake Hernandez, first appeared in *Sky Island Journal*

"Statistical Insignificance," by Juliana, first appeared in *Echoes Through The Stacks: Celebrating Five Years of Poems Penned at Poetry Evenings at Quince Orchard Library*

"Refugee," by Daniel Skach-Mills, first appeared in *the Living Earth Gatherings*, and was reprinted in

"Bail," by Keith Parsons, first appeared in *Zoetic Press, Apocalypse.*

"Create a Revolution," by Diane Raab, first appeared in Verse-Vertal

POETS' BIOGRAPHIES

Fran Abrams, a resident of Rockville, MD, began writing poetry in 2017 after retiring from her day job as a nonprofit arts administrator. Her poems have been published in numerous journals including *The Delmarva Review,* The *Write Launch*, and *The Orchards Journal*, and in more than twenty anthologies. Her books include the full-length collection, *I Rode the Second Wave: A Feminist Memoir* (2022), and two chapbooks, The Poet Who Loves Pythagoras (2023), and *Arranging Words* (2023). One of her poems was nominated in 2023 by *Gargoyle* for a Pushcart Prize. Abrams also was co-editor of an anthology of poems, including her own, titled *Echoes through the Stacks*, published in 2024. Her fourth book, a collection of Nonet poems, titled *Traveling on the Number Nine Bus*, was published by Kelsay Books in August 2025. Please visit franabramspoetry.com for more.

Casey Zella Andrews (she/her) is a queer poet and teacher who lives in West Medford, Massachusetts, with her partner and young child. Andrews has a BA from Hampshire College, earned a MAT from Simmons College to become a high school English language arts teacher in Boston, and earned an MA in Critical and Creative Thinking from the University of Massachusetts - Boston. Her poetry has most recently been published or is forthcoming in *Aprosexia Lit, J Journal,* and *The Marbled Sigh.*

Edward Baranovsky has published in *Eastern Structures, Haiku Avenue, Lynx Journal, Northern New England Review*, among many others. At 78, he has no full collection, so is still emerging He currently lives in Toronto, Ontario, Canada. Website: https://painterpoet.weebly.com Education: BFA 1969, Rhode Island School of Design, Major in Painting. painterpoet.weebly.com

Beau Beausoleil is a poet and activist based in San Francisco, California. He is the founder of Al-Mutanabbi Street Starts Here, a global arts response to the car bombing in Baghdad, Iraq of the booksellers street in 2007. His most recent poetry books include *How Love Sustains Us* (Barley Books U.K.), The *Killing of George Floyd* (Intermittent Press), *Poems for Ukraine* (Barley Books U.K.), and War News II - 12/9/2023 - 6/3/2024 (fmsbw press), written as a series of daily poems that reveal how deeply the killing in Gaza has entered my life.

Tony Brinkley's poetry, art and translations have appeared in *Mississippi Review, Another Chicago Magazine, Beloit Poetry Journal, Cerise Press, Drunken Boat, Four Centuries, Hinchas de Poesie, Hungarian Review, Mayday, New Review of Literature, Puckerbrush Press, Poetry Salzburg Review*, and many others. Before retirement, Brinkley taught literature at the University of Maine. He is co-editor (with Keith Hanley) of *Romantic Revisions* (Cambridge University Press).

Cindy Buchanan grew up in Alaska, has a B.A. in English from Gonzaga University, and studies poetry with Jeanine Walker in Seattle, Washington. She is a member of two monthly poetry groups, is an avid runner and hiker, and lives in Seattle. Her work has been published in *ONE ART, Hole in the Head Review, The Inflectionist Review*, and other journals. Her poetry has been nominated for Best of the Net. Her chapbook, *Learning to Breathe* (Finishing Line Press), was published in 2023. Find her at cindybuchanan.com

Abby Caplin's poems have appeared in *AGNI, Catamaran, Midwest Quarterly, Moon City Review, North American Review, Salt Hill, Spoon River Poetry Review, The Southampton Review*, and elsewhere. She has been a finalist for the Rash Award in Poetry and The Poetry Box Chapbook Prize, and a nominee for Best New Poets, Best of the Net, and the Pushcart Prize. She is the author of *A Doctor Only Pretends (*2022) and a retired physician in San Francisco. www.abbycaplin.com.

Miguel Mesquita da Cunha was born and lives in Portugal, but he daydreams & writes in French. And, every blue moon, in English. (Some friends mistakenly believe he is a retired diplomat, an accusation he strenuously denies). His previous books were jointly published by two Belgian art centres *(K1L & Exit 11): Parle Feu*, a trilogy with paintings by Brigitte Schùermans: *Tribu, Histoires(s), Fournaise* (2017); *Lettres à l'artiste* (2018); Hodie & semper (2019); *Etoiles* (2020); *Eclairs* (2021), with paintings by Brigitte Schùermans. Two composers, Jaime Reis & João Pedro Oliveira, wrote 'quasi-opera' pieces based upon his texts: *Geometrias do inelidível* (JR), & PI (JPO).

Earthling on Mars is a 21-year-old university student whose work is rooted in a love for art, language, and human connection. Through poetry, she seeks to reach people emotionally by offering reflection, understanding, and healing through art.

Sharon Goodier is a published poet originally from Toronto, now living in a retirement residence in Cambridge, Ontario. She has been writing for over 20 years but mostly focused since retiring from teaching high school in 2009. She was very active as both an organizer and reader at poetry events and readings in Toronto but there are none in Cambridge. She hopes to move back to Toronto soon.

Marijo Grogan is a psychotherapist, writer, and environmental activist. Her poetry and essays have been published in *Braided Way*, *LandSlide*, *Snapdragon*, *Tiferet*, *HerStry*, and *Drought Times* among others. A play *Star Wish* was produced at the Heartland Festival, while National Public Radio featured her essay on adolescent angst. Marijo is a contributing writer to the book *EmbodyKind*. She was nominated for a Women of Achievement and Courage Award from the Michigan Women's Foundation.

Sarah Das Gupta is a writer from Cambridge, UK who started writing a year ago while in the hospital following an accident. She holds a degree in History from the University of London and a Certificate in Education from the University of Hull. Her work has been published in over 150 magazines including *American Writers Review*, *New English Review*; *Perfect Haiku*, *Songs of Eretz*, and *Dipity* whose editor published her first poem. Many years ago in India, she contributed to *The Statesman's* book reviews and the regular feature *The Calcutta Notebook*. Her current ambition at 82 is to have a chapbook published.

Ian Hall was born and reared in the coalfields of southeastern Kentucky. His debut collection, *Creekwater Mansions*, is forthcoming from Eastover Press in early 2026. His work is featured in *Narrative, Mississippi Review, The Journal, American Literary Review,* and elsewhere.

Margaret A. Haberman Her poems have appeared in the Island Journal, the journals *Spiritus* and *Kerning*, and been selected for Poems from Here (hosted by Maine Public Broadcasting and Maine Writers and Publishers Alliance). She was designated as a poet for the project Writing the Land (Maine) assigned to work with two land trusts creating poems reflecting specific trust properties (Androscoggin Land Trust 2022, Kennebunkport Conservation Trust 2023). She has three poems which were chosen by The Poets Corner for the Art and Ekphrastic Poetry Challenge, in conjunction with the Page Gallery, Camden, Maine in 2021, 2022, and 2023. In 2024 she co-authored a book of poems with Meg Weston called *To the Point and Back:Swimming Poems* (self-published).

Joan Harvey's fiction, poetry, essays, and translations have appeared in numerous literary journals, including *Bomb Web Conjunctions*, *Another Chicago Magazine*, and many others. She has been an essayist for the arts and sciences blog *3 Quarks Daily* and has won prizes for both poetry and fiction. A piece she wrote was made into a small opera and performed. She is a graduate of the Jack Kerouac School of Disembodied Poetics and lives in the hills above Boulder, Colorado.

Jake Hernandez is a poet and writer based in New York City. His work explores intimacy, memory, and the quiet intersections between love and loss. Originally from Texas, Jake draws inspiration from both the stillness of the natural world and the pulse of city life, often tracing how silence and connection coexist in modern experience. His poems have appeared in *Sky Island Journal* and *Belladonna's Garden*, among others, and he is currently developing his debut poetry collection, which weaves themes of recovery, tenderness, and self-recognition.

Tamar Jacob's work appears in *Gulf Coast, Glimmer Train, New Ohio Review, Grist, L'Esprit Literary Review,* and elsewhere. My recent poetry appears in *Sunspot Literary Review,* and is forthcoming with *Fjords Review.* My poem "Good Wholesome American Thing" was named Poem of the Month by *MER Literary.* I am also a Katherine Anne Porter Fiction Prize winner.

Hibbah Jarmakani is an Arab-American writer and poet, born to Syrian immigrant parents and raised in Sioux City, Iowa. Her work bridges poetry and lyrical nonfiction, using language as a form of resistance against prevailing media narratives about the Middle East Jarmakani's writing confronts issues of identity, anti-Arab sentiment, and the ongoing violence in regions like Syria and Gaza, while also reflecting on the tension of living in a country that frequently plays a role in such conflicts. Her debut appearance as a writer was in the anthology *We the Interwoven*, and her work has been featured on outlets including *Grayzone News* and *Syriana Analysis*.

Jen Johnson is a writer, photographer, and licensed counselor in North Carolina. Her writing has been published in book chapters, literary journals, and magazines. Jen is the author of *Everyday Mindful Substack* that explores mindfulness, creativity, and nature connection for holding life's challenges in one hand and beauty in the other. Her writing and photography explores themes that include psychological space, place, memory, loss, longing, and the beauty and complexity of the search for home in an ever-changing world.

Jen facilitates Writing as Refuge™ workshops online.

M. Jeanette Kelleher is a poet with an MA in American poetry from Montclair State University and an undergraduate degree in English and creative writing from Washington College. She grew up in Wilmington, Delaware and spent summers visiting family in Maine. She lives in Philadelphia with her two children where she teaches high school English at a Quaker school. Jeanette has had poems published in the *Washington College Review, Philadelphia's Commonweal Gallery, Allium Journal, The Fool's World*, and forthcoming work from *Heart on Our Sleeves Press*. In recent years she has attended the Martha's Vineyard Institute for Creative Writing and the Chesapeake Writers' Conference.

Hannan Khan is a nefelibata, poet, fiction writer and scholar of literature & linguistics from Pakistan. He is the winner of the Native Voices Award 2025 for his poetry collection Isn't Cooked Is Cursed,. His work has appeared in *Failed Haiku, IHRAM Literary Magazine, GravesidePress, SpecPoVerse, Eye To The Telescope, Abyss & Apex, The Headlight Review, The /tɛmz/ Review, The Literary Hatchet, Notch Magazine* & is forthcoming in *Winds Of Asia & Native Voices Anthology*. Poetry is his altar; Fiction, his rebellion. He writes to unsettle, to unearth, to unlace. For a glimpse into his life, find him on Instagram: @hannan.khan.official

Lucia Lam won poetry and creative writing contests at the University of British Columbia and was also a finalist for the Holland Park Press Poetry Competition. She is a frequent contributor to *Queen's Quarterly.*

Kirk Lawson lives in Ulster County, New York surrounded by the Shawangunk mountains. He enjoys poetry as a creative outlet to explore and enhance meaning in living. Publications: *Discretionary Love, Months to Years, Thorn and Bloom, Pulses, Healing Muse, Kaleidoscope Ekphrastic Review, MacQueen's Quinterly and the Mackinow*. Grateful to be on this journey with husband Jim and dog Leo.

Kali Lightfoot is a queer poet living in Salem, MA. She worked as a gym teacher, wilderness ranger, manager at Road Scholar, and then Director of the National Resource Center for Osher Lifelong Learning Institutes. Her poetry has appeared in journals and anthologies, and been nominated for Pushcart prizes by *Lavender Review, Poetry South*; and for Best of the Net by *Star 82 Review*. Her first collection, *Pelted by Flowers* (CavanKerry Press) was named a "Must Read" by the Massachusetts Center for the Book. *Big Band Night at the Good Life Bar* (Moon Pie Press) is her second book.

Julia Lisella's latest collection, *Our Lively Kingdom* (Bordighera Press), was named a finalist in the 2023 Paterson Book Prize and Grand Prize Finalist and Poetry Honorable Mention for the Eric Hoffer Book Award. Other collections are *Always, Terrain*, and *Love Song Hiroshima*. Her work has appeared in The *Common, Ploughshares, Nimrod*, and others. She teaches at Regis College and co-curates the Italian American Writers Association-Boston Reading Series. For more, see www.julialisellapoetry.com

RW Mayer grew up in Southern Oregon and has been an educator in Oregon and Washington. He lives in Seattle, Washington where he reads and writes, and fiddles with the guitar. His poetry has appeared in *Breatheveryone.net, The Write Launch, Untenured, The Closed Eye Open, MacQueen's Quinterly*, and others.

Andy McLean is a psychiatrist who has been involved in disaster mental health work. His poetry has been published in numerous literary and medical journals.

Grant Moore is a Senior DevOps Engineer with a background in mathematics and physics. He lives in Cumberland, Maryland. His poetry has appeared in *Macrame Literary Journal* and The Genre Society. He was recognized as a runner-up in the 94th Annual Writer's Digest Writing Competition and had an honorable mention in the Marroween 2025 Contest for *Marrow Magazine*.

Katerina Musienko finds joy in the unpredictable journey of writing. For her, poetry begins as an act of discovery, where each line unfolds into something unexpected and true. Her work explores the intersections of womanhood, immigration, and the quiet act of observing a world full of beauty and complexity. Katerina's creative non-fiction piece, "Yarn Over," was published in the *Capital City Press Anthology*. She continues to write toward moments of blissful clarity that emerge from the torturous, yet necessary, act of creation. More examples of her writing and thinking can be found at katetells.com.

Jen OConnor's poetry and fiction are published in numerous journals, including *American Writers Review, London Journal of Fiction, Sinister Wisdom* and *Orchards Poetry Journal.* Her poem *The World Is Too Much For Us* was just published in the *Voices Unbound* Anthology of International Poetry and *ANThropomorphism* published in *Lavender Review* in June. She was finalist in the New Letters magazine 2023 Robert Day contest and won the 2023 Older Writers Grant from the Speculative Literature Foundation for her short story *Second Hand Salvation.* Jen was a finalist in the 2024 Saints & Sinners Literary Festival Short Fiction Contest in New Orleans and her entry, *Second Hand Salvation,* is published in the Festival's anthology. The *Girl Who Would Be King,* her full-length comedy, was a winner of Chicago's Pride Films & Plays Women's Words contest and is published and licensed by Stage Rights. *Taken For A Ride* was published in *Fresh Words Magazine's One-Act Plays. Gayby's Playdate*, winner of the LGBT Festival in Los Angeles, was produced around the country and in Seoul, South Korea.
Jen holds MA and MFA degrees and worked happily for many years at Walt Disney Imagineering in LA.

Judith P. Oppenhiem is originally from El Paso, Texas. Currently, she lives in Friendswood, TX. These days, she divides her time between the Thursday Afternoon Book Club, League of Women Voters of the Bay Area (Texas), and the Friendswood Poetry Workshop. Her work has also appeared in two publications: *Unbroken* and the January, 2026 issue of *The Ekphrastic Review.*

Frederick Pollack is the author of two book-length narrative poems, *The Adventure* and *Happyness,* both Story Line Press; the former reissued 2022 by *Red Hen Press. Three collections of shorter poems, A Poverty of Words, WORDS,* (Prolific Press, 2015), *Landscape With Mutant* (Smokestack Books, UK, 2018), *The Beautiful* Losses (Better Than Starbucks Books, September 2023), and *The Liberator* (Survision Books, Ireland, 2024). Pollack has appeared in *Salmagundi, Poetry Salzburg*

Review, The Fish Anthology (Ireland), Magma (UK), Bateau, Fulcrum, Chiron Review, Chicago Quarterly Review, etc.

Kathy Pon: My husband is a third generation farmer, and we live in the middle of an almond orchard. My work has been featured in *Passengers Journal, Canary, RockPaperPoem, The Closed Eye Open* and other places. My chapbook, *Orchard Language* (Finishing Line Press) will be published in September 2025.

Bill Prindle is a poet deepening his voice in the third half of life. His poetry explores the seams between the human and nonhuman worlds. From forest wanderings, surviving today's America, and practicing restorative agriculture, his poetry is both personal and collective,introspective and prophetic, reminiscent and present. His 2025 poetry collection Medicine Cache Under Lichen was published by Finishing Line Press. He hosts the Charlottesville Live Poets Society, has won multiple Poetry Society of Virginia awards, and has been published in several journals and anthologies, including the 2021 *Streetlight Magazine Anthology*. He has studied with Lisa Russ Spahr, Neil Perry, and Gregory Orr, among other great teachers...

Raul Partida is a poet and veteran from Tri-cities WA. His work has been featured in *The Skrews Poetry Syndication*, Issue 006. He holds an Associate of Arts from Highline Community College, where he placed amongst finalists for the annual Student Poetry Contest in 2024. He is enrolled at Western Washington University, living a quiet existence in the city of subdued excitement.

Keith David Parsons is a person who came from West Virginia, lives in Washington, DC and is less conflicted about it than you might think. Believes a poem without a message is like a big hole without spikes at the bottom—why would you dig it? Member of DC Poetry Collective; featured in *iNK BLOTS* Vols. 1, 2. Full-length book *Appalachian Sea Tales* forthcoming.

Diana Raab, MFA, PhD, is a poet, memoirist, teacher, thought-lead leader, and award-winning author of fourteen books. Her work has been widely published and anthologized. She frequently speaks and writes on writing for healing and transformation. She writes for *Psychology Today,*

Media, Sixty and Me, The Good Men Project and many others. Visit: dianaraab.com

Laura Ann Reed is the author of the chapbook Homage to Kafka (Poetry Box, 2025). Her poems have appeared in *Wildness, Humana Obscura, Bicoastal Review, Halfway Down the Stairs, The Ekphrastic Review*, and other journals, as well as in nine anthologies including *Poetry of Presence II* (Grayson Books, 2023) and *The Wonder of Small Things* (Storey Publishing,2023) Reed holds master's degrees in clinical psychology and performing arts, and is a Contributing Editor with The Montréal Review. She was born in Berkeley, California, earning her B.A. from The University of California, Berkeley, which included a year at l'Université Aix-Marseille in France. https://lauraannreed.net/

Chivas Sandage is an award-winning poet and writer based in rural San Marcos, Texas, and rural Northwestern Connecticut. Her poetry is forthcoming or has appeared in the *Texas Observer, Vox Populi, Salmagundi, Southern Humanities Review*, and *Cutthroat*, among others. Sandage won the 2021 Claire Keyes Poetry Award, judged by poet Afaa Michael Weaver, for a group of eight poems. She won second place in the Nuclear Age Peace Foundation's 2022 Barbara Mandigo Kelly Peace Poetry Contest. Sandage is the author of *Hidden Drive* (Antrim House, 2012), a top ten finalist for the Foreword Book of the Year Award in poetry and nominated for a Pushcart Prize. She earned an MFA from Vermont College of Fine Arts and a BA from Bennington College.

Carol J. Scamman was born in Massachusetts. With stopovers in NH, PA, NY, and LA, she wound her way to Nacogdoches, TX and shares heart and home with two Siberian Forest cats. She's a retired academic librarian who earned degrees from Grove City College (BA) and UAlbany (MLS). Her poetry has appeared in *Trolley: the online journal of the NYS Writers Institute, rhizomag;* and; *rainy weather days: A defiant literary magazine*. She won second place in her public library's 2022 National Poetry Month Contest and has published creative nonfiction in the anthology, *The West That Was*
carolscamman.com.

Born in Coeur d'Alene, Idaho, **Daniel Skach-Mills** holds a BA from Marylhurst University, and an MAfrom St. Martin's University, Lacey, Washington. Daniel's poems have appeared in *Amethyst*

Review,Sojourners, Soul Forte, Christian Century, The Christian Science Monitor, Sufi (Featured Poet), *Braided Way, Open Spaces, and Kosmos Journal.* His book, *The Hut Beneath the Pine: Tea Poems* was a 2012 Oregon Book Award finalist. In 2018, *The Beyond Within: The Downtown Dao of Lan Su Chinese Garden* was a finalist in The Body, Mind, Spirit Book Awards, and The National Indie Excellence Awards. A former Trappist monk, Daniel lives with his husband in Portland, Oregon, where he served fifteen years as a docent for Lan Su Chinese Garden.

Juliana Schifferes is a local poet from Washington, DC. Her poetry has been published in *Washington Writers Publishing House, The Mid-Atlantic Review, Poetry X Hunger, Poetic Hill* and *Wishbone Words.*

Sharon Scholl is a retired college teacher who convenes a poetry critique group and maintains a website (freeprintmusic.com) that donates her original composition to small, liberal churches. Her poetry collections, *Seasons, Remains, Classifieds, Ghosts,* are available via Amazon Books. Her poems are current in *The Bluebird Word* and *Abandoned Mine.*

In bearing witness, *Peter Gregg Slater* is carrying on a family tradition. His Russian grandparents opposed the Czar, his parents were Old Left, and he was New Left. He participated in the Berkeley Free Speech Movement, anti-Vietnam War protests (being arrested at one), and the founding of the Peace and Freedom Party. At one time an English major, he jumped ship to become a historian. He has taught history at several institutions, including Dartmouth College and the University of California, Berkeley. His work has appeared in *DASH, Workers Write, The Satirist, Masque & Spectacle,* and *WordSwell.*

Cooper Smith is a writer based in Flagstaff, Arizona. He writes from the vast and varied landscapes of Arizona and the Colorado Plateau. His writing explores the intersection of place, time, and self with our experience of the world. His work has appeared in *AZ Daily Sun* and *Deep Wild Journal.*

Ori Z Soltes teaches at Georgetown University across a range of disciplines, from art history and theology to philosophy and political history. His poetry has appeared in a handful of journals, and in several collections. My most recent books of poetry are *Then and Now: Love Lost and Sometimes Found* (Canal Street Books) and *The Poppy Poems: My Life As a Dog.*

Alison Carb Sussman has published the poetry collection *Black Wool Cape* and a chapbook, *On the Edge.* Coming in 2027 from Unsolicited Press are the chapbook *The Sun King,* and a debut novella-in-stories, *The Book of Soldiers.* She won the 2015 Abroad Writers' Conference/ Finishing Line Press Authors Poetry Contest, was highly commended by the 2024 international Moth Poetry Prize, and was a finalist in other contests. Her poetry has appeared in numerous anthologies and publications, including *Atlanta Review, Gargoyle, The New York Times, Rattle, Southword,* and many other small presses and online. She has a BA from Sarah Lawrence College, an MA in Journalism from New York University, and has studied poetry in many workshops, including Geoffrey Nutter's Wallson Glass Poetry Sessions, The Writers Studio, the Writer's Voice, and The New School. Her nonfiction has appeared in newspapers, magazines, and library reference books.

Emily Teitsworth is the Executive Director of a climate and energy-focused nonprofit in the San Francisco Bay Area, and a consultant on issues of gender and racial equity and organizational development. She has been writing actively since the age of six, and studied poetry with David Young at Oberlin College. Emily's poetry has been published in journals including *Nostos, West Marin Review, Artemis, Fireweed,* and *Cathexis Northwest.* Outside of her poetry practice, Emily's writing and commentary has been published widely, including in *Stanford Social Innovation Review* and *The Guardian.*

Rodrigo Toscano is a poet living in New Orleans. He is the author of twelve books of poetry. His latest three books are *WHITMAN. CANNONBALL. PUEBLA* (a National Poetry Series finalist), *The Cut Point, The Charm & The Dread.* His other books include, *In Range, Explosion Rocks Springfield, Deck of Deeds, Collapsible Poetics Theater, To Leveling Swerve, Platform, Partisans,* and *The Disparities.* His poetry has appeared in over 20 anthologies, including, *Best American Poetry* (2023, 2004), and *Best American Experimental Poetry* (BAX). His *Collapsible Poetics Theater* was a National Poetry Series selection. His poetry has appeared in *the Boston Review, Poetry Magazine, The Bennington Review, The Kenyon Review, The Harvard Advocate, Georgia Review, Yale Review, Conduit,* and *Fence.* Toscano works for the

Labor Institute on educational training projects that involve environmental and labor justice culture transformation. rodrigotoscano.com

Joan White's poems have been published in *Cider Press Review, NPR's On Being blog, Abstract Magazine, Burningword Literary Journal*, and *The Nature of Our Times* anthology, among others. Her book, *A Commoner's Prayer*, is forthcoming in April 2026 from Rootstock Publishers. A practicing Zen Buddhist for more than thirty years, she is a student at the Vermont Zen Center where she edits the publication, Walking Mountains, and offers seasonal workshops in haiku. She draws inspiration for her poetry from her work in social justice philanthropy, wandering in the woods and wetlands, and reading about space/time.

Lesley Younge is a multi-genre writer, poet, and middle school educator living in Silver Spring, Maryland. Her work has been supported by *Poetry, MQR Mixtape, Midnight & Indigo, West Trade Review, Full Bleed*, VCCA, the Hurston/Wright Foundation, Anaphora Literary Arts, and others. She is also the author of two books for young people: *Nearer My Freedom*, an award winning verse novel remix of Olaudah Equiano's autobiography, and *A-Train Allen*, her first picture book. Two children's books on the nonviolent life of Reverend James M. Lawson are forthcoming. teacherlesley.com

Tara Zafft is a poet whose work explores themes of motherhood, belonging, war, and personal and collective trauma. Her work has appeared in anthology, *Rumors Secrets and Lies, Poems about Abortion, Pregnancy and Choice, Write-Haus, Aether Avenue Press, The San Diego Poetry Annual, Vita and the Woolf Literary Journal*, and *Dumbo Press*. In 2024, she was awarded the Moonlit Getaway Poetry Prize. Tara holds a BA in Russian Literature from UC San Diego and a Ph.D. in Modern Languages from the University of Bath, UK.

www.ingramcontent.com/pod-product-compliance
Lightning Source LLC
Chambersburg PA
CBHW020418150626
46554CB00014B/1935